J. B. E. Turner MA

D1439949

First published by James Brodie Ltd,
This edition published 1977 by Pan Books Ltd,
Cavaye Place, London SW10 9PG

6 7 8 9

© J. B. E. Turner
ISBN 0 330 50093 7
Printed and bound in Great Britain by
Richard Clay (The Chaucer Press) Ltd, Bungay, Suffolk

Contents

The author

The following outline of Jane Austen's life is based on her letters, and on the books written about her by her nephew, and his son and grandson.

Jane was born in 1775 at the parsonage of Steventon in Hampshire, where her father was rector. She had six brothers and one sister, Cassandra, whom she adored: 'Their attachment was never interrupted or weakened; they lived in the same home, and shared the same bedroom till separated by death.' The two girls were sent to Oxford for a year, when Jane was only seven, to be educated by the widow of a principal of Brasenose, and shortly afterwards to the Abbey School, Reading. Jane was really still too young for this school, but she could not be separated from Cassandra. At the age of nine Jane finished school and completed her education at home.

The family life of the Austens was agreeable and affectionate, full of lively conversation and unspoilt by disagreements. Though not rich, all the children were well educated, and the Austens were able to entertain and to mingle with the best society of the neighbourhood. The days were passed in visits to relations and friends, sometimes as far away as Bath, London and Kent. Jane's letters are full of references to the Balls she has attended at the monthly assemblies at Basingstoke. There are references to tea parties and card-playing, to drives and theatricals, and much news of her two sailor brothers who later became admirals.

Very early Jane began filling copy-books with stories, and in 1796 she started *First Impressions* which later was revised and renamed *Pride and Prejudice*. *Sense and Sensibility* was begun in 1797, and *Northanger Abbey* in 1798. Then comes a gap of some ten years in her literary career, explained in the following ways: as the result of personal griefs over the loss of relations and friends; due to the disappointment caused by being unable to get her works published; and owing to the fact that she had no settled home, moving in turn from Steventon to Bath, Clifton, Adlestrop, Stoneleigh Abbey, Southampton, and to Chawton in 1809.

The next six years at Chawton were the most important of her life. Her earlier novels, *Sense and Sensibility* and *Pride and Prejudice*, were published. *Mansfield Park* was finished in 1813, and published at eighteen shillings a copy in May 1814, and sold out by the autumn. *Emma* was finished in 1815, dedicated to the Prince Regent, an admirer of Jane's work, and published the same year. *Persuasion* was also published in this year.

Her method of writing at Chawton is best described in this passage from her nephew's *Memoirs*.

Most of her work must have been done in the common sitting-room, subject to all kinds of casual interruptions. She was careful that her occupation should not be suspected by servants, or visitors, or any person beyond her own family party. She wrote upon small sheets of paper which could easily be put away, or covered with a piece of blotting paper. There was, between the front door and the offices, a swing door which creaked when it was opened; but she objected to having this little inconvenience remedied, because it gave her notice when anyone was coming.

This hatred of publicity also accounts for the anonymous publication of all her novels.

We are told that she eagerly read the literature of the eighteenth century; delighted in the beauties of nature; played the piano and sang sweetly, and that she was very neat-handed at writing and sewing. She lived entirely apart from the contemporary literary world and probably was never in the company of anyone more talented than herself. Her person is described for us by a niece

The figure tall and slight, but not drooping; well balanced, as was proved by her quick firm step. Her complexion of that rare sort which seems the particular property of light brunettes; a mottled skin, not fair, but perfectly clear and healthy; the fine naturally curling hair, neither light nor dark; the bright hazel eyes to match, and the rather small, but well-shaped, nose.

After nursing her brother, Henry, through a dangerous illness in 1815, her own health suffered, and continued to fail until, in 1817, she was obliged to move to Winchester to seek the best medical advice. A temporary rally was not sustained, and on 18 July she died, and was buried in Winchester Cathedral.

Further reading

Jane Austen: Bicentenary Essays, ed. Halperin (CUP)
Jane Austen and her World, Laski (Thames and Hudson)
Jane Austen's Achievement, ed. McMaster (Macmillan Press)
Critical Essays on Jane Austen, ed. Southam (Routledge & Kegan Paul)

The book

Plot

The story takes place at Mansfield Park in the county of Northampton. Lady Bertram has two sisters, a Mrs Norris, whose husband, the Rev. Mr Norris, has been given the living of Mansfield by Sir Thomas Bertram; and Mrs Price, married to a lieutenant of Marines and bringing up eight children in poverty at Portsmouth. To relieve Mrs Price, the Bertrams adopt her eldest daughter, Fanny, a fragile and shy little girl of ten. Fanny arrives at Mansfield, meets her two aunts, her uncle, and her four cousins, Tom, Edmund, Maria and Julia Bertram. The two girls ignore her and Aunt Norris bullies her, so that she is utterly miserable until, after a week, Edmund finds her crying on the stairs, comforts her and helps her to write to her favourite brother, William. With Edmund's continued kindness Fanny's life at Mansfield improves and she grows up quite happily, helping Lady Bertram.

On the death of Mr Norris, Aunt Norris moves into the village, and Dr Grant and his wife come to the parsonage. Much to the relief of his daughters, who find him rather a martinet, Sir Thomas is compelled to visit Antigua on business and takes Tom with him to separate him from his idle friends. In his absence Maria becomes engaged to James Rushworth, the wealthy heir to Sotherton Court; and Mr and Miss Crawford, step-brother and sister to Mrs Grant, come to stay at the parsonage. Henry Crawford is a confessed flirt, and his sister Mary a rather forward young lady, intent on finding a well-to-do husband. Henry loses little time in flirting with the Miss Bertrams, preferring Maria, although she is engaged. Mary

Crawford at first favours Tom Bertram, but later comes to prefer Edmund, who soon falls in love with her. To complicate the love issue further, Fanny falls in love with Edmund. A visit is made to Sotherton Court for Henry to advise James Rushworth on improving the grounds. During this visit Mary Crawford makes it quite plain to Edmund that she disapproves of his intention of entering the Church.

Meanwhile Tom Bertram returns from Antigua and with a friend, John Yates, decides to produce a play at Mansfield. In spite of Edmund's opposition the scheme goes ahead; an unsuitable play, *Lovers' Vows*, is chosen and after many difficulties the cast is picked. Even Edmund elects to act, much to Fanny's dismay, to save Mary Crawford from playing opposite a stranger. Rehearsals begin and Henry and Maria use them as an excuse to flirt. In the middle of the final rehearsal, Sir Thomas unexpectedly returns, and there is no more play-acting in the house. Henry Crawford, who has raised Maria's hopes of a proposal, now dashes them by announcing his departure for Bath. To show her independence Maria at once marries Rushworth, and Julia accompanies her sister on her honeymoon and then to her new home.

Fanny's importance is increased by her cousins' departure and she is asked to dine at the Grants. Henry Crawford is present and, attracted by Fanny's beauty, decides to flirt with her for a fortnight to pass the time. William spends his leave from the Navy at Mansfield, and Fanny's joy at being with her brother so attracts Henry that he prolongs his stay indefinitely. Sir Thomas gives a 'coming-out' ball for Fanny which she enjoys in spite of the ordeal of being the leading figure. Edmund fears that Mary will never marry him when he is a clergyman; nevertheless, he sets off next day for Peterborough to be ordained. William and Henry depart for London the same day.

When Henry returns to the parsonage he tells his sister that he is determined to marry Fanny, and he is quite certain that she will accept him. During his stay in London, he has arranged for William's promotion to lieutenant, and he now gives this joyful news to Fanny and follows it by proposing to her. She is most distressed at this as she considers he is only teasing her, and when he persists she refuses him. The next day Sir Thomas comes to Fanny's room and tells her of Henry's request for her hand in marriage. Fanny declares she cannot marry him as she does not love him. Sir Thomas is most surprised and accuses her of selfishness and ingratitude. Fanny is miserable for many days. Henry continues to pay his attentions to her. Edmund, still hoping to win Mary, encourages Fanny to love Henry. Mary herself pays a visit to Fanny to persuade her to marry her brother. But all in vain. Sir Thomas, believing that a change might help, arranges for Fanny to stay at Portsmouth with her own family. She spends a rather unhappy three months in her badly-run home amongst her badly brought-up brothers and sisters. Henry Crawford pays her a two-day visit and she notices a great improvement in him. He returns to London. News then reaches Fanny of Tom Bertram's illness, and shortly afterwards comes the terrible report of Henry Crawford's elopement with Maria and of John Yates's with Julia.

Edmund fetches Fanny and her sister, Susan, back to Mansfield. She finds a very distressed family, and the story now hastens to its conclusion. Maria lives with Henry for a time until they hate each other, then she leaves him and lives in another county with her Aunt Norris. John Yates and Julia are repentant and are gradually accepted into the family. Edmund interviews Mary Crawford and to his surprise she makes excuses for her brother's behaviour. His eyes are opened; he leaves her for ever, and she goes to live with Mrs Grant in London. Eventually Edmund learns to forget her and to love Fanny. They marry and take over Mansfield parsonage when the Grants move to London; and so the story ends happily for those who deserve the author's blessing.

Setting

The following facts are gathered from *Mansfield Park* on various aspects of the life of those times; but it must be remembered that only a section (though it represented a large section then) of English life is described in the novel – the life of the country gentry of the professional middle-class, seen through the eyes of an author with essentially feminine interests.

Education

The Bertrams had a nanny, a governess, and 'proper masters'. The following subjects are mentioned: English History, which certainly included the dates of the Kings and Queens of England and the principal events of their reigns; Roman History, including the dates of the Emperors; geography, with such exercises as fitting the map of Europe together and learning the names of the principal rivers; metals, semi-metals, and planets – learning their names; philosophers – learning their names; Scripture, French, music, and art. As will be seen, a large part of education consisted in learning by heart, and though Maria and Julia become distinguished for their *accomplishments*, Sir Thomas deplores the fact that the expensive education which he had given them had been directed only to their understanding and manners and not to their characters.

Entertainment and recreation

Leisure-hour occupations mentioned in the novel are: reading, letter-writing, music, singing, play-acting, card-playing, needlework, dancing, riding, hunting and shooting. Maria and Julia play Fanny a duet her first day; and when Sir Thomas returns from Antigua, he calls for music from his daughters. Mary Crawford plays the harp, and when imagining the accomplishments of the Miss Owens, she guesses: 'Two play on the pianoforte, and one on the harp, and all sing'. Glee-singing was another popular way of spending the evening. The long, chatty letters in the book tell of happy hours spent in writing them, though it is hinted that this is mainly a feminine pastime! Reading aloud is indulged in, and Henry Crawford enthrals his audience with a reading from Shakespeare. The Park has a billiard room, though Tom considers it 'a horribly vile' table! Fanny plays cribbage with Aunt Bertram; whist and speculation are also played, and during a Ball whist-tables are made-up for the older guests – the ladies playing for half-a-crown, and the gentlemen for half-a-guinea stakes.

But the Ball is the height of entertainment and two of them are described. The first is a small one with only five couples dancing to the music provided by a violinist from the servants' hall. The second is Fanny's 'coming-out' Ball, a far grander affair, with twelve or fourteen couples of dancers. After very formal introductions, Fanny leads off with Henry; the chaperons sit together; card-tables are made-up for some; supper is taken, and the dancing is still going strongly at three a.m.

As for outdoor sports, all the younger ones ride and some hunt. Henry Crawford considers himself too old to hunt more than three times a week. Tom and Edmund bring home six brace of pheasants after a day's shooting, and William spends the last day of his leave snipe-shooting.

The clergy

The two types of 'gentlemen clergy' of that age are plainly contrasted in the novel. Mary Crawford speaks of clergymen as having 'nothing to do but be slovenly and selfish', and Henry expects Edmund to live away from his parish and to give sermons only at Christmas and Easter. Edmund, however, is an example of the more serious type of clergyman, whose zeal was inspired by the influence of Wesley and the Methodists. He considers that a clergyman 'has the charge of all that is of the first importance to mankind', and he certainly intends to occupy the parsonage and look after his flock.

Houses and gardens

In the eighteenth century the formal style of William and Anne, with its patterned walks and shaped yews, gave way to a love of the picturesque, with natural scenes of parks and grass slopes. Unfortunately the change went too far and beautiful avenues were cut down and artificial 'ruins' were erected, and even dead trees 'planted', to lend an air of 'naturalness'. The alterations involved in such a change were known as 'improving', and *Mansfield Park* contains references to the 'improvement' of Sotherton Court, of Compton, and of the parsonage at Thornton Lacey.

We are told little of Mansfield Park itself, except that it was a spacious, modern-built house, and that the park was five miles round. There are lawns, gardens, plantations, and a gravel-pathed shrubbery. Sotherton Court is described more fully. After passing the lodge gates, the house is approached from the east by a mile drive through a well-timbered park. It is too lowly situated to command good views. Behind the house is a half-mile avenue of oaks, and running up to the house are lawns with pheasants on them and flower-beds and shrubs. A bowling-green borders the lawn, and beyond that is a terrace-walk, backed by iron palisades, commanding a view of the 'wilderness', a two-acre wood planted with larch, laurel and beech. The whole consisted of about seven hundred acres excluding the water-meadows.

'The house was built in Elizabeth's time, and is a large, regular brick building – heavy, but respectable looking, and has many good rooms.' The rooms are 'all lofty, and many large, and amply furnished in the taste of fifty years back, with shining floors, solid mahogany, rich damask, marble, gilding and carving, each handsome in its way. Of pictures there were abundance and some few good'. The chapel was a spacious, oblong room, furnished in mahogany with crimson velvet cushions and a gallery.

Marriage

Before 'coming-out', at about the age of eighteen, a girl should be with a governess, should look demure, wear a close bonnet, and not a veil, nor carry a parasol, and never say a word in company. She should not dine away from home. Before becoming engaged, she must attend a proper number of Balls with her admirer, and it was not done for him to write to her. (Mary Crawford always included Henry's messages to Fanny in her letters.) During the eighteenth century many marriages among the upper and middle classes were 'arranged', with money or social position as the object. Love as a basis for marriage was just beginning to be accepted as the rule rather than the exception in Jane Austen's time. In *Mansfield Park*, Mary Crawford is determined to marry well, and money is her recipe for a happy marriage. Maria Bertram marries for wealth and position, and her father, though anxious for her happiness, allows the marriage, thinking of the social advantages of the match. When he tries to persuade Fanny to marry Henry, he is thinking of the material advantage of such a match, and overlooks the fact that Fanny cannot love Henry.

Travel

The following journeys are mentioned in *Mansfield Park*. Fanny's first journey by public *stagecoach* from Portsmouth to London, and, after staying the night, by the same means to Northampton, where she was met by Mrs Norris in one of the Bertrams' carriages.

Henry and William *travel post* with four horses to London, from where William continues by stage-coach to Portsmouth. (Travelling 'post' was a system introduced in the middle of the eighteenth century. It consisted of either hiring a fresh coach and horses at each stage of the journey, or of using the traveller's own coach throughout and hiring only the horses at each stage.)

Fanny and William travel post to Portsmouth in February. They start in Sir Thomas's carriage, but change that and the horses at the first stage. They pass through Oxford and stay the night at Newbury, leaving early the next morning and arriving at Portsmouth before dark.

Edmund travels from London to Portsmouth by *the mail*. (Palmer's mail coaches were introduced at the end of the eighteenth century. They carried four persons as well as the letters.)

Edmund takes Fanny and Susan back from Portsmouth to Mansfield by post, staying the night at Oxford and reaching Mansfield the next day.

The ten-mile trip to Sotherton is made in Henry's *barouche*, an open four-wheeled coach, seating four (facing in pairs) with a high driving seat, or *box*, holding two. This, a delightful carriage for the summer, is preferred to Lady Bertram's *post-chaise*, which was a closed carriage seating three, facing forwards, with the driver mounted.

Whilst at Sotherton, Mr Rushworth suggests touring his estate in his *curricle*, a two-wheeled, stylish carriage, drawn by two horses; but this is turned down as it only holds two persons.

The discomforts of winter travel are illustrated in the description of Lady Bertram's and Mrs Norris's journey to Sotherton. They used four horses with the coachman on the driving-seat (which suggests it was a coach and not the post-chaise) and a groom astride the leaders. But the roads were so bad they thought they would never get through, and Mrs Norris walks up one hill to save the horses.

Mrs Rushworth travels to Bath in her *chariot*, which is like a post-chaise, with the addition of a box for the driver.

Long journeys were also made on horseback. Edmund rides to Sotherton and back, and also to Peterborough to be ordained.

Characters

Fanny Price

She is as good a little creature as ever lived, and has a great deal of feeling

The eldest daughter of Mrs Price was aged ten when she came to Mansfield Park to be adopted by Sir Thomas and Lady Bertram. She was 'small for her age, with no glow of complexion, nor any other striking beauty; exceedingly timid and shy, and shrinking from notice; but her air, though awkward, was not vulgar, her voice was sweet, and when she spoke her countenance was pretty'. Her shyness was probably a result of her mother's preference for sons and indifference to daughters, and the atmosphere at Mansfield Park no doubt aggravated it: Mrs Norris bullied her; Sir Thomas frightened her; her cousins, with the exception of Edmund, treated her with disdain, and Lady Bertram, though kind, was too lazy to try to understand her. It is not surprising that she begins by sobbing herself to sleep every night for a week, until Edmund pities her, comforts her and, continuing in his kindness, enables her to grow up not unhappily for the next eight years at Mansfield.

Her position as helper to Lady Bertram does not rid her of a sense of inferiority. 'I can never be important to anyone,' she says, and she listened to her cousins' accounts of their social festivities, 'but thought too lowly of her own situation to imagine she would ever be admitted to the same'. She was not often invited into the conversation of others and 'her thoughts and reflections were habitually her best companions'. The east room becomes hers when no longer needed as a school-room, and there she often retires to her books and her hobbies, and to seek comfort when her intentions have been misunderstood or her feelings disregarded. There she retires after Tom and others have tried to persuade her to take part in the play, much against her will. Further comment on her dislike of publicity comes from Mary Crawford when she says Fanny was 'almost as fearful of notice and praise as other women were of neglect'.

Fanny is extremely sensitive, and many are the occasions when she is filled with 'alarms and embarrassments'. Sir Thomas's unexpected return from Antigua causes alarm to most, but Fanny's exceeded all – she nearly faints. Before the Ball given in her honour, 'she had too many agitations and fears to have half the enjoyment in anticipation which she ought to have had'. When Henry brings her news of William's promotion, and, at the same time proposes to her, 'she was feeling, thinking, trembling, about everything; agitated, happy, miserable, infinitely obliged, absolutely angry'. The subsequent interviews with Henry and with Sir Thomas, about her refusal of Henry, cause her infinite pain and confusion. On arriving at Portsmouth to stay with her family, 'Fanny was all agitation and flutter – all hope and apprehension', and when Henry Crawford pays her a visit there, she is terrified and 'fancied herself on the point of fainting away'. The news of Henry's elopement with Maria stupefies her with horror: 'The night was totally sleepless. She passed only from feelings of sickness to shudderings of horror; and from hot fits of fever to cold.'

This extreme sensitiveness, combined with an unselfish nature, leads her to feel most strongly for other people in their troubles. She alone feels sorry for Julia in her bad-tempered outburst of jealousy. Being sorry for Mr Rushworth, she kind-heartedly tries to teach him his lines in the play. Her great alarm at Sir Thomas's sudden return is increased by pity for his feelings at discovering his family acting without his knowledge. She is intensely sympathetic towards Edmund, when Sir

Thomas finds out that he has taken part in the play. In all her misery, caused by the persistence of Henry's attentions, she is still able to spare a thought for him, and is distressed to think that he may be miserable too. When she leaves for Portsmouth, she does not like to think how Lady Bertram will miss her. The news of Tom's illness and the subsequent report of the elopements fill her with pity for the Bertrams.

Fanny has high principles and a serious mind, and timid though she is, she is not afraid to support her champion, Edmund, in his defence of the clergy, and in his disapproval of an ill-chosen play. When she came to believe that Edmund, whom she secretly loved, would marry Mary, she showed 'all the heroism of principle, and was determined to do her duty' by trying to overcome 'all that bordered on selfishness, in her affection for Edmund'. Her high principles are further illustrated by her great distress at Henry's flirting with the engaged Maria, and by the pain caused to her by her father's oaths and his partiality for spirits. Her disgust at Mary Crawford's mercenary motives when inquiring about Tom's illness is another example.

Sometimes her fault-finding is not so justified, and when she and Edmund criticize some seemingly harmless remarks of Mary's about her uncle, they both seem to find a rather priggish enjoyment in doing so. When Fanny reads *Lovers' Vows* for the first time and runs through it 'with an eagerness which was suspended only by intervals of astonishment', one cannot help suspecting that she was looking forward to the objections that Edmund must make to the play.

Fanny, nevertheless, is always ready to criticize her own motives. She is relieved when Sir Thomas goes abroad, but ashamed of being so, and tells herself she is ungrateful. After refusing to take part in the play, she questions herself as to whether she was being selfish in giving way to her fears of publicity. She even reproaches herself for 'some little want of attention' to her bullying Aunt Norris. When Sir Thomas accuses her of obstinacy, selfishness and ingratitude in refusing Henry's proposal, she is utterly miserable and uncertain as to the amount of truth in his harsh words.

In spite of her physical frailty, which makes her tired very easily, she is a great help to Lady Bertram, who soon depends on her for everything. As she grows up her looks improve and Sir Thomas, on his return, comments on her prettiness; Henry later finds her 'absolutely pretty', and Edmund eventually learns to prefer her 'soft light eyes to sparkling dark ones'.

Timidity, anxiety and doubt are not characteristics that by themselves endear a heroine to the reader, and in Fanny they predominate. We may not all agree with Jane Austen in her apparent preference for 'My Fanny' above her other heroines; we may at times even lose patience with this girl who, rather than face up to life, prefers to hide behind others or to retire to her room. Accustomed, perhaps, to the more robust heroines of a later age, we may not admire so much 'tenderness of disposition', such 'incurable' gentleness. Nevertheless, in criticizing her for shrinking from difficulties, we must take into consideration the nature of those difficulties. Taken at an early age from her own family, and placed in the midst of a family who, with one exception, lack either the ability or the inclination to understand her, she falls in love with the only one who attempts to help her and suffers most on his account, keeping her love secret and bearing all the pain of hearing his declarations of love for another.

Fanny surely deserves our sympathy, if not our love – 'She is as good a little creature as ever lived, and has a great deal of feeling.'

Edmund Bertram

His strong good sense and uprightness of mind

Edmund, the younger son of Sir Thomas and Lady Bertram, was educated at Eton and Oxford and destined for the

Church. Unlike his brothers and sisters, he seems to have inherited his father's seriousness and sense of decorum. We are told that 'his strong good sense and uprightness of mind, bid most fairly for utility, honour, and happiness to himself and all his connections'.

Fanny is treated rather disdainfully by her other cousins, but Edmund is full of sympathy, kindness, and understanding. At the end of her first week at Mansfield, he finds her crying and, by helping her to write to her favourite brother, soon comforts her. He sees that she has a horse to ride, as it is good for her health, and he acts very unselfishly in offering to stay at home in order to let Fanny go to Sotherton with the others. He is, in fact, 'always true to her interests, and considerate of her feelings . . . giving her advice, consolation, and encouragement'.

When the pretty and entertaining Miss Crawford comes to live at the parsonage, his sensitive nature soon falls to her charms; and his sincere, simple love, running counter to the forwardness of this young lady, frequently causes his heart to ache and his judgement to err. Mary, in spite of her worldliness, feels the charm of his sincerity, steadiness and integrity. In her criticisms of the clergy, she draws from Edmund an honest, patient, and sensible defence of his vocation.

Edmund, however, is not perfect. He is rather too ready to find fault, and when Mary speaks somewhat lightly of her uncle, the Admiral, referring to him as 'not the first favourite in the world', he and Fanny are quick to discuss, in self-righteous tones, her 'very indecorous' behaviour.

In judging Edmund's attitude to the play, the stricter family life of those times must be considered, and each of his objections treated separately. Firstly, he objects strongly to any play being acted, giving as his reasons the lack of feeling it would show to his father, who was absent and possibly in danger, and the lack of prudence in such an activity whilst Maria was engaged. Today these reasons might not appear sufficiently strong to save Edmund from being considered at least a 'spoil-sport', but family discipline has changed, and it must also be remembered that Edmund must have known that his sister Maria was flirting with Henry in spite of her engagement to Rushworth, and that she would welcome any further opportunities to continue flirting. Secondly, Edmund objects to the choice of *Lovers' Vows* as 'exceedingly unfit for private representation', and here his censure seems even more justified. (See note on *Lovers' Vows*.)

The events which follow his attempt to prevent the play and his absolute refusal to take part in it are not to his credit. He hears that Mary Crawford is to act and is 'obliged to acknowledge that the charm of acting might well carry fascination to the mind of genius'. Then he hears that they propose to ask an outsider to take the part of Anhalt, to whom Mary, as Amelia, would have to declare her love. In an interview with Fanny, Edmund declares he will now take the part of Anhalt in order to save Mary from the embarrassment of playing opposite an unknown young man. Fanny is astounded by his inconsistency and the reader must surely suspect him of self-deception and sympathize with his brother and sister in their opinion that 'he was driven to it by the force of selfish inclinations only'.

His reason seems to be blinded by his love for Mary, and this is again evident in his attitude to Fanny concerning her refusal of Henry Crawford. He urges her to marry him against her will. He excuses Crawford's earlier flirting all too easily by saying that Maria provoked it, and rather betrays his motives when he admits that he has an interest in the match; for he can only see how completely desirable it would be if his beloved Fanny were to marry the brother of his adored Mary.

After Henry's disgraceful elopement with Maria, Edmund visits Mary in London. He is appalled by her attitude: she looks upon the affair as mere folly and deplores the detection rather than the sin. He unburdens his mind to Fanny and declares: 'The charm is broken. My eyes are opened'. He suffers his punishment for the self-deception incurred under the charms of Mary Crawford, and when his anguish has worn away, and when he has ceased regretting Mary, he learns 'to prefer soft light eyes to sparkling dark ones', and marries Fanny.

Henry Crawford

Thoughtless and selfish from prosperity and bad example.

Henry Crawford owned an estate in Norfolk worth £4,000 a year. He was brought up by his uncle, the Admiral, who delighted in him but spoilt him; as Henry says himself, 'few fathers would have let me have my own way half so much'. It is not surprising, then, that Henry is an independent character who dislikes 'a permanence of abode or limitation of society'.

A very charming young man, not handsome, but well-built and attractive, his attitude to women also shows a lack of constancy. Mary, his sister, says, 'he is the most horrible flirt that can be imagined. If your Miss Bertrams do not like to have their hearts broke, let them avoid Henry'. Her words are soon proved, for he loses little time in flirting with Maria and Julia, and admits his preference for the elder, although she is engaged. When Henry leaves Mansfield to return to Norfolk, the Miss Bertrams find life very dull and Henry ought to have stayed away, 'had he been more in the habit of examining his own motives, and of reflecting to what the indulgence of his idle vanity was tending; but thoughtless and selfish from prosperity and bad example, he would not look beyond the present moment', and he returns after a fortnight to continue trifling with the affections of the sisters.

The preparation for *Lovers' Vows* gives him ample opportunity for this, and Maria, who intends to play Agatha, is quick to ensure that he shall play Frederick, thus arousing Julia's intense jealousy. Rushworth is treated shamelessly by Henry and Maria, who rehearse their scene together an unnecessary number of times. When Sir Thomas's return cuts short the last rehearsal, Henry retains Maria's hand and she is certain that he will declare his love for her; but when he calls next day, it is to announce his departure for Bath; 'and so ended all the hopes his selfish vanity had raised in Maria and Julia Bertram'.

When Henry next returns to Mansfield, he plans to 'amuse' himself for a fortnight by making Fanny fall in love with him. 'I cannot be satisfied without making a small hole in Fanny Price's heart.' Then William comes to stay on leave and Henry has moral taste enough to appreciate the happy reunion of brother and sister. In her joy, Fanny's attractiveness so increases that Henry becomes more interested in her than he had foreseen, and he decides to prolong his stay indefinitely. Henry, who began by flirting with Fanny for amusement, now falls in love with her. After the Ball, he tells his sister that he is determined to marry Fanny, and so great is his vanity that he is certain she will accept him. He procures William's promotion and after greeting Fanny with the joyful news, he proposes. She considers it all as mere trifling but her refusal strengthens his resolve to win her. 'He had been apt to gain hearts too easily. His situation was new and animating.' And so in spite of her obvious distress, he continues to woo her and his excessive vanity makes him confident of success. When he visits Fanny at Portsmouth it seems almost possible that he will succeed. He is kind, considerate, and behaves with great charm to the Prices. Fanny fancies a wonderful improvement in him. Then, instead of returning from Portsmouth to Norfolk, curiosity, vanity, and immediate pleasure are too much for him and he stays in London to meet Maria. This is his undoing – 'Henry Crawford, ruined by early independence and bad domestic example, indulged in the freaks of a cold-blooded vanity a little too long'. He elopes with Maria.

His punishment comes swiftly; they live together until Maria hates him and until he feels she has ruined the happiness he might have had with Fanny, and we leave him full of remorse for the opportunity lost through his selfish love of pleasure, his lack of constancy, and above all, his vanity.

Mary Crawford

Matrimony was her object, provided she could marry well.

After the death of her aunt, Mary Crawford came to stay at the Mansfield parsonage with her half-sister, Mrs Grant. She had lived in London with her aunt and her uncle, the admiral, since the death of her mother, and being used to London society, she is a little apprehensive as to whether a country parsonage will suit her. She is remarkably pretty and very entertaining, and the combination of her beauty, wit and good-humour soon causes Edmund to fall in love with her.

She is well-off with £20,000 and, making matrimony her object, provided she can marry well, she is at first attracted by Mrs Grant's suggestion of the elder Bertram as a husband, but soon comes to prefer his younger brother Edmund. Her views on marriage betray a somewhat cynical nature, and the outspoken way in which she gives them is one of the many examples of her intolerance: 'My dear Mrs Grant, there is not one in a hundred of either sex who is not taken in when they marry'. Her recipe for a happy marriage is a large income.

Her opinion of the clergy illustrates even more plainly her worldliness, with its cynicism, and the almost arrogant confidence of her judgement. 'A clergyman is nothing', and again 'a clergyman has nothing to do but to be slovenly and selfish'. Her views on family prayers are similarly disparaging: she pictures the belles of Sotherton 'starched up into seeming piety, but with heads full of something very different, especially if the poor chaplain were not worth looking at'.

She is, however, capable of kindness and affection as is best shown in her defence of Fanny against Mrs Norris's cruel attack on her for not taking part in the play: 'I do not like my situation; this *place* is too hot for me,' says Mary, moving away from Mrs Norris and close to Fanny to comfort her. Her single-hearted love for her brother and the affection she feels for Edmund, which leads her to regret her harsh criticism of the clergy, must also be to her credit.

This affection for Edmund seems genuine enough, for she is not a little jealous of the Miss Owens when he prolongs his stay with that family; but it is an extremely selfish affection, for she does her utmost to persuade him against being a clergyman. '*Lord* Edmund or *Sir* Edmund sounds delightfully', but she has little use for Mr Edmund, and even less for the Rev. Edmund. And so it is that, when Tom Bertram is seriously ill, she writes to Fanny for news of his progress without disguising her shameful hopes that Edmund will gain wealth and consequence by his brother's death. She had just received Edmund coolly in London, but now she is anxious for his next visit, and Fanny's surmise seems justified: 'Edmund would be forgiven for being a clergyman, it seemed, under certain conditions of wealth . . . She had learned to think nothing of consequence but money.'

At the close of the story, after her attempts to make light of her brother's disgraceful conduct, Edmund's eyes are opened, and he says, 'Hers are faults of principle, Fanny – of blunted delicacy and a corrupted, vitiated mind.' A stern judgement. Is he justified? She has shown herself worldly, dogmatic, selfish, and cynical on the one hand; but very sociable and capable of kindness and affection on the other. What evidence is there of her lack of principle?

The gift to Fanny of a necklace before the Ball shows a certain lack of honesty. She deceives her into believing it is just a gift from her, when in fact she and Henry have schemed to ensure its place on Fanny's neck. Out of curiosity she persuades Henry to stay in London for a party to which she has invited Maria Rushworth, and the origin of his subsequent elopement can be traced to this culpable curiosity of Mary's. She gives Maria credit for sending her husband to Bath and so getting him out of the way while she enjoys herself. Finally, she treats her brother's crime as a mere folly, and in her defence of his elopement with a married woman appears to Edmund to regret the detection rather than the crime.

Tired of the friends who had misled her, tired of ambition and vanity, she eventually finds comfort in her sister's kindness and the tranquillity of her ways, but is long in finding 'anyone who could satisfy the better taste she had acquired at Mansfield, whose character and manners could authorize a hope of the domestic happiness she had there learned to estimate, or put Edmund Bertram sufficiently out of her head'.

Sir Thomas Bertram

There was never much laughing in his presence.

Sir Thomas Bertram, as undisputed head of the house, has at his best a fine and dignified manner, and at his worst a pompous and short-sighted nature. His ability to control the members of his household is well illustrated by the way in which he immediately stops the rehearsals of *Lovers' Vows*, an action which is criticized alone by a comparative stranger to the house, Mr Yates, who finds him, 'Unintelligibly moral and infamously tyrannical'.

As a parent, Sir Thomas is not a success. He is anxious to do right by his children, but his reserved manner and lack of affection form a barrier to any mutual understanding. When he departs for the West Indies, Maria and Julia are delighted; when he returns, Mansfield Park becomes 'all sameness and gloom' compared with the months of his absence. There was never much laughing in his presence.

In condoning the marriage of Maria to Rushworth, he allows the material advantage of such a match to outweigh considerations of his daughter's happiness, and it is only after the subsequent desertion and elopement that he becomes conscious of his shortcomings as a parent and is filled with remorse at his selfish motives. He realizes then that his severity to his children has checked their spirits and driven them to seek comfort from Mrs Norris who spoils them.

His attitude to Fanny shows the same well-meaning intention with its accompanied lack of understanding. On her arrival at Mansfield Park, he is determined to be the real and consistent patron of Fanny, and to do his duty by her; but he is also anxious to make her remember that she is not a Miss Bertram. He sees she needs encouragement and tries to help, but again he is handicapped by his over-serious nature; as Henry Crawford says, he is kind to Fanny in his way – 'but it is the way of a rich, superior, long-worded, arbitrary uncle'. Nevertheless, kind he is on many occasions, such as his return from the West Indies when he has a special welcome for her, or when Mrs Norris spitefully arranges for her to walk, rather than drive, to her first dinner party, and he at once orders his carriage for her. He is generous too in giving a Ball to please her and her brother, and on another occasion he is amazed that she has not been given a fire in her room.

It is when interviewing Fanny about her rejection of Henry Crawford's proposal of marriage that we see his lack of understanding and his prejudice. The match appears to him a highly convenient arrangement and, treating Fanny first with calm displeasure, he praises Henry's attractions. Then with cold severity he accuses her of being wilful, perverse, lacking in deference to those who could advise her, and in consideration for her own family, who would have rejoiced in the marriage. Only her tears prevent him from prolonging an accusation of ingratitude. However, in spite of such harsh words, his kindness is still apparent, for on leaving this interview, he at once makes arrangements for her to have a fire in her room, and when later Mrs Norris expresses much the same sentiments about Fanny as he had in the interview, he inwardly considers her most unjust.

At the end of the story, after much suffering, the better side of

Sir Thomas's nature prevails: he realizes he is sick of ambitious and mercenary connections, and 'prizing more and more the sterling good of principle and temper', he welcomes the marriage of Fanny to his younger son Edmund.

Lady Bertram

The picture of health, wealth, ease and tranquillity.

Thirty years before the story begins, Miss Maria Ward of Huntingdon married Sir Thomas Bertram of Mansfield Park, Northampton, and as a baronet's lady had 'all the comforts and consequences of a handsome house and large income'. A prosperous and beautiful woman, beauty and wealth were all that excited her respect. Very early we are told that she was 'a woman of very tranquil feelings, and a temper remarkably easy and indolent... She spends her days sitting nicely dressed on a sofa, doing some long piece of needlework, of little use and no beauty; thinking more of her pug than her children, but very indulgent to the latter when it did not put herself to inconvenience; guided in everything important by Sir Thomas, and in smaller concerns by her sister'.

It is not surprising then that she paid little attention to the upbringing of her daughters and that she was even too lazy to accompany them on public occasions. Even her husband, on his departure abroad, realizes that she is not capable of performing her duties to them. He is right. She has no idea of the nature of the play they rehearse in his absence, and when Edmund describes it as 'exceedingly unfit', she characteristically dismisses her responsibility with the words 'Do not act anything improper, my dear, Sir Thomas would not like it. – Fanny, ring the bell; I must have my dinner.'

She is completely self-interested. She had no fears for Sir Thomas's safety in the West Indies – 'being one of those persons who think nothing can be dangerous, or difficult, or fatiguing to anybody but themselves'. Later when Tom speaks of the play as a good means of cheering their mother in her 'very anxious period', they all look towards her – 'sunk back in one corner of the sofa, the picture of health, wealth, ease and tranquillity' – while Fanny does the work!

In her attitude to Fanny, we see her selfishness at its worst, though, unlike Mrs Norris, she is never intentionally unkind to her. Her chief worry on adopting Fanny is – 'I hope she will not tease my poor pug'. However, she soon finds Fanny's usefulness in the house a further aid to her own indolence and is most loath to do without her even if it means pleasure for Fanny. She says she cannot spare her to visit Sotherton with the others, nor, later in the story, to dine for the first time at the Grants. Indifferent to her own daughters' education, it is not surprising that her advice to Fanny to accept Henry Crawford's proposal of marriage was almost the only piece of advice she had given her in eight and a half years. When Fanny returns from her stay at Portsmouth, and after all the tragic events that have happened in her absence, Lady Bertram's greeting is typical of her self-interestedness – 'Dear Fanny! now I shall be comfortable.' But, in defence of her, we must remember that Fanny too is delighted to be back and to be of help to an aunt who, though helplessly lazy and sublimely unconscious of it, has, nevertheless, never been intentionally unkind to her.

At the close of the story, Lady Bertram's nature remains unchanged. She finds it possible to relinquish Fanny to Edmund, not in the interest of a son's and niece's happiness, but because she now has Susan Price to wait on her.

Mrs Norris

Her love of money was equal to her love of directing.

Miss Ward, a sister of Lady Bertram, married the Rev Mr Norris who had scarcely any private fortune, but was given the living of Mansfield by Sir Thomas Bertram. It is Mrs Norris who suggests adopting Fanny but, though happily believing she is therefore the most liberal-minded sister and aunt in the world, she has not the least intention of being at any expense in her maintenance. She refuses to have her at the parsonage, and later when Mr Norris dies she moves into a house in the village, chosen for its smallness to avoid having to have Fanny.

She is a self-important busybody. When Sir Thomas is in the West Indies, she indulges in baseless fears for his safety and revels in preparing tragic announcements for his family. She is delighted with the idea of the play – it gives her a reason for bustle and importance and obliges her to live at Mansfield at others' expense. She is far too busy superintending the details of costumes, etc, for the play, to keep an eye on her nieces. When Sir Thomas returns, she is thoroughly upset because the unexpectedness of his arrival has deprived her of the importance of preparing for him and of announcing his arrival. She tries – 'to be in a bustle without having anything to bustle about'.

She spoils Maria and Julia and is full of self-praise for her efforts in bringing about the marriage of Maria to Mr Rushworth, looking upon it as a personal triumph and showing little insight of her niece's character. When a Ball is to be given, she enjoys the importance of doing the honours of the evening and begins by rearranging and spoiling the fine fire the butler has prepared.

She practises economy to the extent of meanness, and speaks of herself as a poor desolate widow with barely enough to make both ends meet; until Lady Bertram reminds her of her income of £600 a year. Her only comment on William's promotion is that it would save Sir Thomas money and make some difference in her own presents too. She returns from the visit to Sotherton with a lapful of edibles she has 'sponged', and after the play is abandoned she makes off with the curtain!

She bullies Fanny throughout the story, treating her as very much beneath her cousins and determined to keep her beneath them. Fanny is very distressed when she hears she may have to live with an aunt who has never been kind to her. Mrs Norris tries to prevent Fanny from visiting Sotherton with the others. She disapproves of a Ball being given for her, and she it was who forbade her to have a fire in her room. She is beastly to Fanny when the latter begs not to be given a part in *Lovers' Vows* – 'I shall think her a very obstinate, ungrateful girl if she does not do what her aunt and cousins wish her – very ungrateful indeed, considering who and what she is.' She is just as beastly to her on the occasion of her invitation to dine out for the first time, at the Grants' – 'there is no real occasion for your going into company in this sort of way . . . The compliment is intended to your uncle and aunt and me.' Then she entreats Fanny not to put herself forward (the last thing Fanny would do) – 'Remember, wherever you are, you must be the lowest and the last.'

Towards the end Sir Thomas begins to realize that she is 'one of those well-meaning people who are always doing mistaken and very disagreeable things', and at the end he feels her 'an hourly evil'.

After the downfall of her nieces to which she had contributed by her excessive indulgence and flattery, she is 'an altered creature – quieted, stupefied', and no help to anyone. Finally she leaves Mansfield, regretted by no one, and lives with Maria in another county.

Maria and Julia Bertram

Had no idea of carrying their obliging manners to the sacrifice of any real pleasure.

Daughters of a stern father and an indolent mother, the Miss Bertrams were brought up at Mansfield Park under the instruction of a governess and the spoiling influence of Aunt Norris. The instruction gave them brilliant acquirements, elegance, and naturally easy manners; the spoiling encouraged their vanity and selfishness; they believed they had no faults, and they 'had no idea of carrying their obliging manners to the sacrifice of any real pleasure' for the sake of others. Their father was no object of love to them and they welcomed his departure as freeing them for every indulgence. At twenty-one Maria considers matrimony a duty, and as Rushworth could give her a larger income than her father's and a house in town, it became her duty to marry him.

Henry Crawford brings out the worst in the sisters; they both fall for him – Maria in spite of her engagement to Rushworth. On the drive to Sotherton, Julia is delighted to gain the seat on the box with Henry, whilst her sister sulks in the carriage. Arriving at Sotherton, Maria attaches herself to Henry and Julia is left to talk with Mrs Rushworth. Her want of self-command, of a just consideration for others, of the knowledge of her own heart, and of the principle of right made her miserable.

During the rehearsals of *Lovers' Vows*, Maria behaves disgracefully to her fiancé. She arranges for Henry to play Frederick and takes every opportunity of flirting with him and of avoiding Rushworth. Julia's jealousy is aroused; first she loses her temper, then she either sits in silence or ridicules the acting. The unwelcome return of Sir Thomas is softened for Maria by her certainty that Henry is about to propose to her; but the following day Henry announces his departure for Bath, 'and so ended all the hopes his selfish vanity had roused in Maria and Julia'. Partly to show her independence of Henry, and partly to escape the restraining influence of Mansfield Park, Maria marries Rushworth at once and Julia goes to stay with them.

Then comes the news of Maria's elopement with Henry and Julia's with John Yates. Sir Thomas, though suspecting a lack of principle in his daughters, blames their upbringing to a certain extent. They had never been taught to govern their inclinations and tempers by a sense of duty. 'To be distinguished for elegance and accomplishments – the authorized object of their youth' was not enough.

Maria lives with Henry, hoping to marry him, until, disillusioned, she learns to hate him and, leaving him, lives with Mrs Norris in another county, where 'their tempers became their mutual punishment'.

Julia's fate is better, owing to her more favourable disposition and to not having been spoilt to the same extent by the flattery of Mrs Norris. 'Her temper was naturally the easier of the two; her feelings, though quick, were more controllable; and education had not given her so very hurtful a degree of self-consequence.' She had married Yates mainly to avoid returning to Mansfield Park and to the dreaded anger of her father at her sister's conduct. She is humble and wishes to be forgiven, and her husband is anxious to be accepted by her family.

Tom Bertram

Born only for expense and enjoyment.

The sort of young man to be generally liked; he was gay, agreeable and gallant, but he felt born only for expense and enjoyment. His carelessness and extravagance gave Sir Thomas much uneasiness, and prevented Edmund taking the living of Mansfield Park when Mr Norris died. His father takes him to Antigua with him to separate him from bad friends. On his return, Tom, aided by his idle friend Yates, is the prime mover of an unsuitable play. Tom frequently stays away from Mansfield and indulges in many parties and race meetings. It is whilst at Newmarket that a neglected fall leads to his serious illness and the doctor's fearing for his lungs. However, his health improves and with it his character. He becomes useful to his father, steady, quiet and unselfish.

James Rushworth

A very stupid fellow.

'If this man had not twelve thousand a year, he would be a very stupid fellow,' says Edmund of him, and his conduct throughout the story proves the truth of Edmund's assertion. His sole topic of conversation at dinner is the 'improvement' of Sotherton Court, but when the Bertrams and Crawfords visit his estate, he has no ideas of his own on the subject. During the rehearsals for the play, he thinks only of his fine clothes and his forty-two speeches, though there is little hope of his being able to learn these. Sir Thomas soon discovers that he is 'an inferior young man, as ignorant in business as in books, with opinions in general unfixed, and without seeming much aware of it himself'. He allows Maria to treat him shamefully during their engagement, and suffers the indignities of stupidity when, shortly after their marriage, she leaves him for Henry.

John Yates

Not much to recommend him.

The Hon. John Yates, we are told, had 'not much to recommend him beyond habits of fashion and expense'. Tom Bertram met him at Weymouth and invited him to Mansfield. The choice of *Lovers' Vows* is mainly due to his having taken part in it before. He is vain about his own abilities as an actor, and when Sir Thomas returns and stops the play, he shows so little appreciation of Sir Thomas's character that he prolongs a conversation on the rehearsals. Sir Thomas knows enough of his family and connections to consider his presence extremely unwelcome, and is delighted when he leaves. Julia allows his attentions both at Mansfield and in London, and, as a result of her sister's conduct, she elopes and marries him. In the end, he is anxious to be received into the Bertram family and prepared to be guided by Sir Thomas. Though not very solid, there seems to be a hope of his becoming less trifling and more domesticated.

William Price

Courage and cheerfulness.

Fanny's elder brother is her favourite, and quite understandably. He is a likeable young man with an open, pleasant countenance, and frank, unstudied, but feeling and respectful manners. He visits Fanny at Mansfield before going to sea as a midshipman in HMS *Antwerp*, and again after seven years' service. Sir Thomas then finds him a young man 'of good principles, professional knowledge, energy, courage and cheerfulness'. He is commissioned as second lieutenant of HM Sloop *Thrush*, and after spending his ten days' leave at Mansfield, he takes Fanny back to Portsmouth before sailing. At the end of the story we hear of his continued good conduct and rising fame.

Mr Price

He swore and he drank, he was dirty and gross.

Fanny's father, a disabled lieutenant of Marines, enters late in the story with an oath and a smell of spirits. He neglects his family in favour of his dockyard acquaintances and has no interests or knowledge beyond his profession. When Fanny comes to stay he scarcely notices her except to make her the object of a coarse joke. He is not an attractive character.

Mrs Price

Her days were spent in a kind of slow bustle.

Frances Ward, a sister of Lady Bertram, married Lieutenant Price of the Marines and raised nine children in comparative poverty. She resembled Lady Bertram in having an indolent character; her house was badly managed; her children out-of-hand. After nine years she greets Fanny kindly enough, but is full of worries and complaints: there is no butcher in the street and so no meal to await them; she wishes the bell were mended; she apologizes for the fire; the tea is long overdue and the noise and confusion terrible. Practically her only topic of conversation is the inefficiency of Portsmouth servants. As a parent she is not unkind, but favours her sons and has little interest in her daughters except for Betsey, whom she spoils. Her days are spent in a 'slow bustle', and in vain attempts to manage her children and servants.

Dr Grant

The doctor was very fond of eating.

On the death of the Rev. Mr Norris, Dr Grant takes the living at Mansfield and enters the parsonage. He is a gentleman, a good scholar, and often preaches good sermons, but he is indolent and very fond of eating and continually nags his wife about the food. Eventually he leaves Mansfield, having succeeded to a stall in Westminster, and dies of apoplexy after three great institutionary dinners in one week.

Mrs Grant

Her usual good humour.

The wife of Dr Grant is a woman of pleasant manners and cheerful temperament. When the Crawfords come to stay, she finds considerable enjoyment in planning their marriages to the Bertrams. She offers to sit with Lady Bertram all day to enable Edmund and Fanny to go to Sotherton, and with her usual good humour agrees to take part in the play. When they move to London, Mary Crawford makes a permanent home with her.

Mrs Rushworth (Senior)

A well-meaning, civil, prosing, pompous woman.

The mother of James Rushworth is 'a well-meaning, civil, prosing, pompous woman, who thought nothing of consequence but as it related to her own and her son's concern'.

Susan Price

Susan tried to be useful.

Fanny's younger sister is a determined girl, anxious to set her muddled home right without knowing how to do so. She becomes very fond of Fanny and, returning with her to Mansfield, she takes her sister's place as Lady Bertram's comforter, when Fanny marries. Her usefulness, gratitude and sweet temper endear her to the Bertrams.

Betsey Price

A spoilt child.

Fanny's five-year-old sister is a spoilt mother's darling who is left with the servants too frequently and encouraged to tell tales about them.

Style

A relation of Jane Austen writes of her invincibility at 'spilikins'. This is not so irrelevant as it may seem in an account of her style, for the requirements of that old-fashioned game – precision and 'an infinite capacity for taking pains' – are two of the chief requirements for writing a novel like *Mansfield Park*. Jane Austen adds to these her own genius, which includes a lively sense of humour and a pleasantly malicious sense of fun.

Her choice of characters is limited: they come from one class and have one code of behaviour. Her selection of incidents is limited: very little happens in the story. Her interpretation of human emotions is also limited; there is no ugly hatred, no burning revenge, no passionate love. She spoke herself of the 'little bit of ivory' on which she painted 'with so fine a brush', and frequently her work has been compared to an exquisite miniature. Within her limits she has achieved perfection, and it is fortunate for the English novel that she fully appreciated her limits and refused on more than one occasion to be tempted to write of other subjects than those she understood so intimately.

Humour, slightly malicious but never irrelevant and always entertaining, is the most noticeable feature of her style. The characters of Mrs Norris and Lady Bertram are built up by the frequent little sallies of penetrating wit made at their expense. Jane's humour is a part of her writing and not just a diversion. Mrs Norris's attitude to the adoption of Fanny is soon summed up by 'Nobody knew better how to dictate liberality to others'. We are told that she 'consoled herself for the loss of her husband by considering that she could do very well without him'. Her 'busybody' nature is crystallized in the reference to the new arrivals, the Grants: 'They had their faults, and Mrs Norris soon found them out'. Her tendency to gossip is unforgettably illustrated in the reference to Maria's engagement to James Rushworth, when she was 'talking of it everywhere as a matter not to be talked of at present'. A more subtle thrust is made in the controversy as to the cause of Fanny's headache. Mrs Norris has just suggested that she caught it whilst picking roses in the heat, for Lady Bertram; the latter then casually mentions that Fanny has twice been on an errand for Mrs Norris. ' "What!" cried Edmund, ". . . walking across the hot park to your house, and doing it twice, ma'am? No wonder her head aches." Mrs Norris was talking to Julia and did not hear.' In the same way Lady Bertram's delightful indolence and captivating self-interest are etched on the reader's memory by the author's wit, with its measure of acid. 'I hope she will not tease my poor pug', is my Lady's reaction to the adoption of a niece. Best of all perhaps, the scene when Tom, to overcome Edmund's opposition to theatricals, urges that it would be a means of easing his mother's anxiety during the weeks of Sir Thomas's absence: ' "It is a *very* anxious period for her." As he said this, each looked towards their mother. Lady Bertram, sunk back in one corner of the sofa, the picture of health, wealth, ease and tranquillity, was just falling into a gentle doze, while Fanny was getting through the few difficulties of her work for her.' Lady Bertram's rapid shouldering and unshouldering of her duty to her children – ' "Do not act anything improper, my dear," said Lady Bertram; "Sir Thomas would not like it – Fanny, ring the bell; I must have my dinner" ' – reminds us of another occasion where the author uses an abrupt change of subject to provide comic relief. Mrs Price has just heard the report of Maria's elopement. ' "Indeed, I hope it is not true," said Mrs Price plaintively; "it would be so very shocking! – If I have spoken once to Rebecca about that carpet, I am sure I have spoke at least a dozen times." ' The novel is inlaid with such satirical gems and one more example must suffice. It is Maria's wedding: 'It was a very proper wedding. The bride was elegantly dressed – the two bridesmaids were duly inferior – her father gave her away – her mother stood with salts in her hand, expecting to be agitated – her aunt tried to cry – and the service was impressively read by Dr Grant.'

Irony is a frequently recurring feature of the novel. Sir Thomas, on his return from Antigua, congratulates himself on his luck in finding his family 'all collected together exactly as he could have wished'. Little does he know yet what has collected them together! The whole relationship between Fanny and Edmund in full of irony. She is in love with him, but he, ignorant of this, tries to persuade her to love Henry.

Jane Austen has an excellent sense of the dramatic. Sir Thomas's return is well hidden, and the surprise is perfect and leads to a fine climax when he and Yates come face to face on the stage. The dialogue is natural and each character keeps his or her individual manner of speech.

Great attention is paid to detail, as in the description of Fanny's room, or as in the discussion as to whether Fanny should accept her first invitation to dine out.

Contrast is usefully employed whether in character, as between Fanny and Mary Crawford, or in atmosphere, as between Mansfield Park and Portsmouth.

The use of letters towards the end of the book brings variety to the telling of the story, and they are good letters, ranging from the typically chatty style of Mary Crawford to Edmund's serious epistle. The inclusion of letters in a novel was no innovation; in fact, Samuel Richardson (1689–1761), who is usually considered the earliest English novelist, set a fashion by writing the whole of his stories in the form of letters. It is interesting therefore to note that Jane Austen wrote her first stories as a series of letters. 'I have now attained the true art of letter-writing,' she said, 'which we are always told is to express on paper exactly what one would say to the same person by word of mouth.'

All these are just features of style which, combined with great care in composition and revision, and inspired by her genius, produce a book which places her among our greatest novelists.

Lovers' Vows

A full understanding of Chapters XIV to XIX depends largely on a knowledge of the play chosen by the party at Mansfield to produce in Sir Thomas's absence. A résumé of its plot may also help us to determine whether Fanny and Edmund were justified in opposing its performance. Edmund, it must be remembered, was opposed to any play being produced, but particularly critical of *Lovers' Vows*, which he considered exceedingly unfit, and Fanny, after reading the play, is astonished that it should have been chosen.

The play was written by Kotzebue, a German dramatist, and adapted by Mrs Inchbald about 1800. It was performed in England and the frequent number of reprints show how popular it was.

Characters

BARON WILDENHEIM	John Yates
COUNT CASSEL	James Rushworth
ANHALT	Edmund Bertram
FREDERICK	Henry Crawford
VERDUN THE BUTLER	Tom Bertram
AGATHA	Maria Bertram
AMELIA WILDENHEIM	Mary Crawford
COTTAGER	Tom Bertram
COTTAGER'S WIFE	Mrs Grant

Landlord, Countryman, Country Girl, Huntsmen and Servants.

(We are not told who took the minor parts, though we know that Tom Bertram had several small parts.)

The plot

When the curtain rises AGATHA is being turned out of an inn by the landlord as she has no money. FREDERICK, a soldier on leave, arrives at the inn, sees Agatha and, to his surprise recognizes her as his mother. They embrace. (*This and further embraces in the first Act would account for Maria's wish to play Agatha to Henry's Frederick, and also for the unnecessary number of rehearsals of Act I!*) Frederick then explains his reason for returning – his regiment require his birth certificate. In some confusion, Agatha explains that he has none, as he is the natural son of a Baron Wildenheim who seduced her whilst she was in service at his castle nearby. (*Hardly a suitable topic for a family play in these days, and even less in those times of greater strictness.*) Frederick then finds lodging for them both in a cottage. The COTTAGER and the COTTAGER's WIFE tell them that Baron Wildenheim's wife has died and that he has returned to live in the castle.

In the next scene we see BARON WILDENHEIM and his daughter AMELIA, who is being courted by COUNT CASSEL, a ridiculous fop. She, however, is in love with her tutor, ANHALT, who now enters. The Baron declares his dislike of Count Cassel for his lack of heart and brains and asks Anhalt to educate him and also to instruct Amelia in matrimony.

The Baron and the Count go shooting, and Frederick, who is penniless, unsuccessfully attempts to hold up the Baron, little knowing that he is his father. He is overpowered and imprisoned in the castle.

Amelia, undergoing instruction in matrimony from Anhalt, declares her love for him in an outspoken manner. (*This scene probably prompted Fanny to consider the character of Amelia as totally improper for home representation; and Julia, in a temper, to describe the same character as 'an odious, little, pert, unnatural, impudent girl'.*)

The BUTLER enters next and describes the attempted hold-up of the Baron *in rhyme*.

Amelia visits Frederick in prison with a *basket of provisions*; she tells him the name of the Baron and he realizes it is his father.

The Butler, *in rhyme*, discloses to the Baron the fact that Count Cassel is a philanderer and has previously seduced a girl. The Baron dismisses Count Cassel.

Frederick is now brought by Anhalt to the Baron, expecting to suffer death for attacking him. He tells the Baron that he is his son and the amazed Baron sends Anhalt to find Agatha. He promises Frederick he shall be his heir and Agatha shall be given a house nearby. Frederick refuses to accept this unless the Baron marries Agatha. Anhalt advises the marriage and the Baron eventually agrees to this and also to the marriage of Anhalt and Amelia, and the play ends happily.

There is little literary merit in this melodrama, though of course Edmund and Fanny did not condemn it on those grounds. When judging it as a fit play for family representation, we can, I think, sympathize with their censure since the choice seems typical of Mr Yates, who 'had not much to recommend him', and his friends, who were sufficiently known to Sir Thomas to render his introduction to Mansfield 'exceedingly unwelcome'.

Summaries of chapters, textual notes and revision questions

Chapter I

Thirty years before the start of the story, Maria Ward married Sir Thomas Bertram. Her sisters did not do so well for themselves; one married the Rev. Norris, who received from Sir Thomas an income in the living of Mansfield; the other fared worst and, marrying an impecunious Lieutenant of Marines, broke away from her family and raised eight children in poverty. When a ninth was expected, she wrote a conciliatory letter to the Bertrams, and as a result the Bertrams decided to adopt the eldest daughter to relieve the Prices' distress. Sir Thomas is in doubt as to the success of this venture, but Mrs Norris adds her persuasion, and Fanny, aged nine, is sent for.

Huntingdon This county town of Huntingdonshire, fifty-nine miles north of London, was the birthplace of Oliver Cromwell.

Northamptonshire An east-midland county of England whose southern border lies some forty-five miles north-west of London. It is richly cultivated and finely wooded in parts.

Portsmouth A famous naval station seventy-four miles south-west of London in the county of Hampshire. The dockyard was regularly established about 1540, but long before then the town was of importance to the Navy.

Chapter II

Fanny Price arrives at Mansfield Park. She meets Sir Thomas and Lady Bertram, their sons, Tom and Edmund, and their daughters, Maria and Julia. She is afraid of everyone and is taken to bed in tears. The next day the daughters have a holiday from their lessons with Miss Lee, the Governess, in order to get to know Fanny, but they find her 'cheap' as she has not the same number of sashes as they have, and they leave her to herself. When lessons begin again, Miss Lee and the daughters find her ignorant. She is miserable and sobs herself to sleep every night for a week. Then Edmund finds her crying on the attic stairs; is very kind to her and helps her to write to her favourite brother William. Edmund continues in his kindness and Fanny becomes more comfortable and grows up at Mansfield Park, not unhappily. Much to her delight William visits her before going to sea. Meanwhile Edmund has left Eton and gone to Oxford. He is to be a clergyman.

orthography Spelling.
as low as Severus Down to the Emperor Severus who died AD 211.

Chapter III

Three years later Mr Norris dies. Edmund is not old enough to take the living as planned and Sir Thomas, owing to the extravagances of Tom, cannot afford to place a friend temporarily in the Parsonage to hold it for Edmund. Dr Grant therefore takes the living. Mrs Norris as a widow is now expected to take Fanny to live with her. Fanny finds this idea most disagreeable as her aunt constantly bullies her. However, Mrs Norris has no intention of adopting her and has purposely taken the small *White House* in the village to allow no room for Fanny. She tells Lady Bertram of her objections, and no more is heard of the project. Dr and Mrs Grant arrive at the Parsonage. Mrs Norris soon discovers that the Doctor is very fond of eating. A great event – Sir Thomas has to go to Antigua to see to his estate and decides to take Tom with him. Maria and Julia are relieved; so is Fanny but rather ashamedly.

Antigua A very fertile island in the British West Indies whose chief exports are sugar and pineapples. Discovered in 1493 by

Columbus, it remained uninhabited until 1632 when a body of English settlers took possession of it.

Chapter IV

The Miss Bertrams, now fully established among the belles of the neighbourhood, enter into the gaieties of the season, while Fanny, eighteen now, is perfectly happy helping Lady Bertram at home. Her grey pony dies and she suffers from lack of exercise, but Edmund wins her grateful admiration by providing her with a mare. Sir Thomas, due to return that September, is delayed by business and sends Tom back. Maria Bertram becomes engaged to Mr Rushworth, a rich young man who owns Sotherton Court. Mr and Miss Crawford, stepbrother and sister to Mrs Grant, come to stay at the Parsonage. Mrs Grant schemes to marry Mary Crawford to Tom, and Henry Crawford to Julia, but Mary warns her that he is a horrible flirt.

steward Estate manager.
tête-à-tête A private conversation.
protégée One who is under the care of another.

Chapter V

Maria and Julia admire Mary Crawford and both fall for Henry, who finds them most agreeable but hints that he prefers the elder, although she is engaged. This leads to a discussion on marriage between Mrs Grant and Mary. Mary, with an eye on his estate, favours the ideas of Tom Bertram as a husband. There follows a discussion as to whether Fanny is 'out' or not; it is decided that she isn't.

esprit du corps Loyalty (usually *de*).
out See under *Marriage*, p.7

Chapter VI

Tom Bertram leaves for the races. The Crawfords and Rushworth dine at the Park and discuss the latter's intention to improve the grounds of Sotherton Court. Mrs Grant discloses that Henry Crawford has improved his estate at Everingham, and Julia suggests that he should now help Rushworth. He offers his services and Mrs Norris then suggests that they should make up a party to visit Sotherton.

Mr Repton A leading improver of the day.
Moor Park A type of apricot described in 1802 as 'a fine fruit, and ripens about the latter end of August'.
Cowper William Cowper, a poet (1731–1800) who lived for some time at Huntingdon. The quotation comes from *The Task*.
Twickenham Twelve miles from St Paul's Cathedral, London.
barouche See under *Travel*, p.8.
Bath A hundred and seven miles west-by-south of London. The Romans discovered the beneficial nature of the waters there and the Roman Baths are still to be seen. Two royal visits in 1734 and 1738 made Bath a centre of English fashion.
Post-captains Naval captains, a commissioned as opposed to a courtesy title.

Chapter VII

Edmund and Fanny discuss Mary Crawford and condemn her lack of decorum in criticizing her uncle in public. Edmund, however, admires her in all other respects. Mary's harp arrives and Edmund goes to the Parsonage every day to hear her play. He falls in love with her. He arranges for her to share his mare with Fanny. On her second ride with Edmund and others, she is late, and Fanny walking to meet them is rather pained at seeing the happy group, with Edmund paying attention to Mary. For the next four days Mary has the mare and Fanny does not ride. Fanny develops a headache which Edmund in shame ascribes to her lack of riding exercise, but which in fact was mainly due to Fanny feeling not a little neglected.

tambour frame A hoop frame for embroidery.
poor-basket A basket of old clothes to be mended and given to the poor.

Chapter VIII

Mrs Rushworth visits the Park to urge the invitation to Sotherton. Lady Bertram declines to undertake the fatiguing journey. The Miss Bertrams and the Crawfords accept, and Edmund is to go on horseback. Mrs Norris refuses the invitation for Fanny, saying that Lady Bertram cannot spare her. An argument follows as to which carriage to take and Henry's barouche is decided upon. Rather than that Fanny should miss the visit, Edmund decides to stay at home with his mother in spite of the objections of Mrs Norris; but the situation is saved by the offer of Mrs Grant to stay with Lady Bertram, and Fanny and Edmund are to go. Julia wins the coveted seat on the box with Henry, much to Maria's chagrin, but apart from this the ten-mile journey passes without incident.

prosing Chatting or gossiping.
box . . . chaise . . . post-chaise . . . barouche See Travel, p.8.
court-leet and court-baron Assemblies of manorial tenants presided over by the lord or his steward.

Chapter IX

Arriving at Sotherton Court, the party eat a meal and then Mrs Rushworth shows them round the house with its great number of rooms, richly furnished in the style of fifty years back. They enter the chapel and Fanny is disappointed in its lack of grandeur. Mrs Rushworth explains that her husband discontinued the use of the chapel for family prayers. Fanny considers this a pity but Mary Crawford imagines how little the belles and the servants of the house must have enjoyed the services. Edmund comes to Fanny's assistance and defends the use of the chapel. Seeing Maria and Rushworth standing near the altar, Julia declares it to be a pity that Edmund is not yet in orders otherwise he could marry them then and there. Mary is taken aback by the news that Edmund is to enter the Church and apologizes for her previous remarks about the clergy. They all leave the house and go on to a lawn and admire the plants and pheasants. Mr Rushworth, Henry Crawford and Maria discuss improvements. Edmund, Mary Crawford and Fanny wander through the wilderness. Mary questions Edmund on his decision to be a clergyman, saying there was no distinction to be gained in that profession and that he was fit for something better. Edmund defends his chosen vocation at length. Fanny is tired after the walk and the three of them sit on a bench. Mary soon gets up and she and Edmund walk into the wood leaving Fanny sitting alone.

curricle See *Travel*, p.8.

window tax A duty levied on the number of windows in a house. First imposed 1695, and abolished 1851.

"blown by the night wind of heaven" *and* **"Scottish monarch sleeps below"** Quotations from Sir Walter Scott's *Lay of the Last Minstrel*.

wainscot Foreign oak used for panelling. Furniture made of mahogany did not appear in England until about 1730. Mrs Rushworth was wrong in attributing the fittings of the chapel to James II's reign.

Blair's Hugh Blair (1718–1800), a Scottish divine famous for his sermons, published in five volumes.

bon mot A witty saying.

ha-ha A sunken boundary to a garden or park.

Chapter X

Fanny is left alone for twenty minutes and then Maria, Mr Rushworth and Henry join her on the seat. They discuss improvements and decide to move to a knoll in the park for a better view. This necessitates passing through an iron gate which is locked and Mr Rushworth, who has forgotten the key, returns to the house to fetch it. Henry and Maria, rather than wait, pass round the edge of the gate and Fanny is left alone again. Then Julia appears, having escaped from the company of Mrs Rushworth; she too passes round the gate and goes after the others. Five minutes later Mr Rushworth arrives with the key. He is very vexed that they have not waited for him, but Fanny persuades him to follow them. After a long wait Fanny goes in search of Mary and Edmund and finds them; they too had wandered into the park. They return to the house and meet Mrs Rushworth and Mrs Norris. Later the others return and dinner is taken, followed by tea and coffee. Then they drive back, Julia happy again on the box and Mrs Norris with a lapful of spoils she has cadged from the housekeeper and the gardener.

Quarterly Reviews Issues of a Tory periodical founded in 1809.

Revision questions on Chapters I–X

1 Describe Fanny's arrival at Mansfield Park, and her first week there.

2 How did the following people treat Fanny: Mrs Norris, Sir Thomas, and Edmund?

3 What are your first impressions of Henry and Mary Crawford?

4 Describe the house and grounds of Sotherton Court.

5 What do you learn about the characters of Julia and Edmund at Sotherton?

Chapter XI

Much to his daughters' regret, news comes from Sir Thomas that he is to return in November. Edmund will take orders on his return, and this prompts Mary to criticize again his choice of profession, and to pour scorn on the clergy. Edmund makes a logical defence, supported by Fanny. In spite of Mary's harsh words about his future vocation, Edmund gazes after her with ecstatic admiration as she joins the others to sing a glee.

packet Short for packet-boat, which is the mail-boat.
bon vivant One fond of good-living.

Chapter XII

Tom returns from his six-weeks' round of pleasure and Mary is convinced that she prefers Edmund. Henry goes to his estate at Norfolk, but returns after a fortnight. The acquisition of a violinist in the servants' hall leads to a small Ball with no more than five couples dancing, during which Fanny overhears Mrs Norris telling Mrs Rushworth that Henry is likely to marry Julia. Tom Bertram dances with Fanny to avoid playing whist with his aunt and others.

Chapter XIII

John Yates, a friend of Tom's, comes to stay. Previously he had been with Lord Ravenshaw in Cornwall, where the family were prevented from producing a play called *Lovers' Vows* by the death of a grandmother. Tom Bertram's suggestion of producing a play at Mansfield is well received in spite of Edmund's opposition. He considered it would show lack of feeling to Sir Thomas in his danger abroad and imprudence in view of Maria's engagement. Tom then suggests converting the billiard room into a theatre, with the help of Jackson, the carpenter. Edmund, supported by Fanny, perseveres with his opposition but is unable to dissuade his sisters and the news that Mary Crawford will act leaves him in two minds.

after-piece A farce or short piece after the main play.
my name was Norval From a tragedy called *Douglas* by John Home.

Chapter XIV

The construction of the theatre goes ahead, but choosing a play presents difficulties. Some want comedy, others tragedy, but at last Tom suggests *Lovers' Vows*, much to the delight of Yates and the approval of all. Casting proves another very controversial task. Yates is to play *Baron Wildenheim*; Tom Bertram – *The Butler*; Henry Crawford – *Frederick*; Maria and Julia both want to play *Agatha* to Henry's *Frederick*; and Julia, feeling slighted when Henry suggests Maria should have the part, refuses the alternative of playing *Amelia* and leaves the room in a temper. Maria goes to the Parsonage to offer the part of *Amelia* to Mary Crawford. Fanny reads the play and finds it most unsuitable.

Hamlet . . . Macbeth . . . Othello Tragedies by William Shakespeare (1564–1616).
Douglas A romantic tragedy by J. Home, acted in 1756.
The Gamesters A comedy by James Shirley, acted in 1633.
The Rivals and *The School for Scandal* Comedies by R. B. Sheridan, produced in 1775 and 1777 respectively.
Heir at Law A comedy by G. Colman, produced in 1797.

Chapter XV

Mary accepts the part of *Amelia*; Mr Rushworth chooses *Count Cassel* and likes the idea of being finely dressed and having forty-two speeches. Edmund is shocked by the choice of play and entreats Maria not to play *Agatha*. She is adamant however. Mrs Norris then gives a report on her activities in superintending the curtain, which contains much self-praise for her economy. After dinner the Crawfords pay a visit and the lack of a player to take the part of *Anhalt* is discussed. Mary tries in vain to make Edmund take the part. Fanny is urged to take the part of *Cottager's Wife*. She is terrified and nearly in tears after Mrs Norris has tried to bully her into it, but Mary is kind to her. Tom then decides to invite a local acquaintance to play *Anhalt*.

cottages and alehouses Scenery for Act I, *Lovers' Vows*.
crowsfoot Wrinkles at the corner of the eyes.

Chapter XVI

Fanny retires to the east room and reconsiders her refusal to act. This room has become her own and there she keeps her plants and books and all her souvenirs and hobbies. She is beginning to accuse herself of ingratitude and selfishness based on a fear of exposing herself, when Edmund asks to speak to her. He declares his intention to take the part of *Anhalt* after all, in order to avoid the introduction of an outsider – an action which he considers highly objectionable. When Edmund leaves, Fanny is miserable that he should have shown such inconsistency in deciding to take part in a project he had opposed from the start.

transparencies Pictures on a translucent material, stuck on the window.
Tintern Abbey In Monmouthshire, Wales, one of the most famous ecclesiastical ruins in England.
netting-boxes Boxes for a fancy network fabric made with needles.
Lord Macartney George, Lord Macartney (1737–1806). *Plates to his Embassy to China* were published in 1796.
Crabbe's *Tales* George Crabbe (1754–1832), a poet. The *Tales* were twenty-one stories published by him in 1812.
The Idler A series of papers contributed by Samuel Johnson to the *Weekly Gazette*, between 1758 and 1760.

Chapter XVII

Tom and Maria are delighted at their victory over Edmund. Mrs Grant agrees to play *Cottager's Wife*, and though Fanny is thereby relieved, she is jealous that Mary Crawford had instigated this move and, in addition, feels very left out of everything. Julia, besides feeling left out, suffers greatly from being slighted by Henry Crawford and eases her feelings by ridiculing the acting, by flirting with Yates, and by hoping that trouble will come of her sister's attachment to Henry. Everyone else is too busy to notice Julia's discomposure.

Templars Members of a military and religious order founded about 1118 to protect the Holy Sepulchre in Jerusalem.

Chapter XVIII

A period of dissatisfaction. Tom has engaged a scene-painter and invited several families to witness the production; both actions are against Edmund's wishes. Tom frets at waiting for the scenes to be painted and also finds his parts insignificant. Yates is disappointed in Henry Crawford; Tom speaks too quickly; Mrs Grant spoils everything by laughing; Edmund is behindhand in his part; Mr Rushworth continually needs prompting and can get no one to rehearse with him; Maria and Henry rehearse together unnecessarily often and arouse Rushworth's jealousy. Fanny finds pleasure in watching and judges Henry to be the best actor. She tries to teach Rushworth his part and enjoys helping everyone. She is sewing a cloak together in the east room when Mary Crawford knocks and asks if she may rehearse her part with Fanny reading that of *Anhalt*. They are half-way through the scene when Edmund knocks with a similar request. Mary and Edmund now rehearse together and Fanny prompts. The first regular rehearsal of the first three acts has just begun with Fanny reading the part of *Cottager's Wife* for Mrs Grant, who cannot come, when suddenly Julia throws open the door and announces that Sir Thomas has returned.

éclat Publicity.

Chapter XIX

The news of Sir Thomas's return fills most of the actors with horror. His sons and daughters go to meet him, Maria comforted in this crisis by the pressure of Henry's hand. The Crawfords return to the Parsonage and, after a short delay, Fanny, thoroughly agitated, leaves Yates alone on the stage and goes to pay her respects to Sir Thomas. He gives her a particularly warm greeting and then sitting round the fire, they all listen to the story of his voyage. Lady Bertram is delighted to have him back, but Mrs Norris feels she has been deprived of the delight of 'managing' his arrival. Lady Bertram, to the concern of her children, mentions the play, but Tom changes the conversation to pheasant shooting. After tea Sir Thomas goes to look in his room. Tom, hearing that Yates is all alone, goes to the theatre and arrives in time to see Sir Thomas, on entering the stage by the library door, come face to face with a ranting Yates. Tom hurries to introduce Yates, but his father, knowing the Yates family, is not impressed. They return to the drawing-room and Sir Thomas would have dropped the topic of the theatre but for Yates's tactless persistence, and in answer to his invitation to a rehearsal, Sir Thomas declares that there will be no more rehearsals. Rushworth declares his dislike of so many rehearsals and, to the amusement of the others, Sir Thomas congratulates him on his judgement.

packet See note p.44.

Chapter XX

Edmund gives his father a complete statement of the acting

scheme and clears Fanny of any blame. Sir Thomas considers it sufficient reproof to forbid any further acting, but hints to Mrs Norris that her acquiescence in the scheme was to be regretted. She turns the conversation on to her praiseworthy economy and on to the engagement of Maria, for which she takes the whole credit and goes on to describe in detail the mid-winter journey with Lady Bertram to Sotherton to further that cause. Sir Thomas removes all traces of the theatre. Mr Yates, attracted by Julia, stays a few days longer. Maria is now expecting Henry to propose to her at any moment and is heart-broken when he comes to say that he is leaving for Bath. She realizes that all her hopes of him are ended. Mr Yates departs and with him the last trace of theatricals at Mansfield.

leaders Leading horses.
éclaircissement A clearing-up of what is obscure, i.e. Henry Crawford's intentions.

Revision questions on Chapters XI–XX

1 Give a detailed description of Fanny's east room.

2 Summarize the argument between Edmund and Mary about the Clergy.

3 Describe the difficulties encountered in choosing the cast for *Lovers' Vows*.

4 Write an account of the effect of Sir Thomas's sudden return.

5 What do the theatricals tell you about the characters of Edmund, Julia, and Maria?

Chapter XXI

The return of Sir Thomas brings monotonous gloom to the house compared with the lively evenings of his absence. Much to Fanny's embarrassment, Edmund tells her that his father admires her prettiness. Sir Thomas is soon disillusioned about Mr Rushworth and offers to help Maria release herself from the engagement, if she wishes it. Maria, smarting from Henry's jilt, determines to marry Rushworth and show Henry her independence. Sir Thomas is not sorry to retain the chance of increased respectability and influence such a marriage would bring. The wedding takes place, and Julia joins them on their honeymoon at Brighton.

Brighton A famous seaside resort, fifty-one miles south of London, which first became fashionable in 1756.

Chapter XXII

Fanny's consequence increases on the departure of her cousins, not only at home but also at the Parsonage, for being caught in the rain one day she was prevailed upon to go in, and stayed some time listening to Mary playing on the harp. A friendship resulting from this visit leads Fanny to call regularly. On one occasion Edmund and Mrs Grant join them in the garden and Mary renews her criticism of Edmund's intention to enter the Church. On departing, Fanny is invited to dine at the Parsonage.

the famous Doge ... In reply to the question, 'What do you find the most remarkable at Versailles?', the Doge said, 'It is to see myself here.' (Voltaire's *Louis XIV*.)

Chapter XXIII

Lady Bertram is surprised at the Grants asking Fanny to dinner and is not sure that she can spare her. Sir Thomas settles the question and orders his carriage for her in spite of Mrs Norris's unkind insistence upon her walking. To their surprise Edmund and Fanny find Henry Crawford has returned to the Parsonage. He pays compliments to Fanny during dinner, but she is angry with him for wishing that Sir Thomas had not returned in time to prevent the play. Henry teases Edmund about the first sermon he will soon be preaching. Mary is upset at being reminded of Edmund's being so soon to take Orders and angry with him for his determination.

menus plaisirs Pocket-money.

Chapter XXIV

Henry decides to stay another fortnight and to pass the time by making Fanny fall in love with him. His continued attentions make her more civil to him, though she still dislikes him for his flirting with Maria, and is in little danger of falling to his advances, owing to her feelings for Edmund. William, still a midshipman but expecting promotion, comes to stay. The reunion of brother and sister is one of mutual joy, and even Henry is touched by the scene, and his admiration for Fanny is so increased by her display of vitality, that he prolongs his visit indefinitely, and lends William one of his hunters.

tout ensemble General effect.

Chapter XXV

Intercourse between the Park and Parsonage is resumed. Sir Thomas cannot help noticing that Henry is an admirer of Fanny. A dinner party at the Parsonage is followed by whist and a round game, Speculation. During a lull in the card-playing, Henry tells of a visit to Thornton Lacey, Edmund's future living, and outlines a plan for improving the parsonage there. He then tells Fanny that he plans to rent that parsonage himself, but this is upset by Edmund's declaration that he intends to live there himself. At the end of the evening, Wil-

liam tells Sir Thomas that he would very much like to see
Fanny dance.

speculation A card game involving the buying and selling of
trump cards.

Chapter XXVI

Sir Thomas is determined to gratify William's wish to see
Fanny dance, and overrides Mrs Norris's objection, and plans
go ahead for a Ball with twelve to fourteen couples. Fanny,
though delighted, is most anxious about her dress and about
wearing an amber cross which William had given her, for
which she has no chain. Edmund, meanwhile, has two serious
problems on his mind – ordination and matrimony. The first is
to take place very shortly; the second depends on Mary Crawford's preferring him to a gay life, and he wonders. Fanny seeks
advice from Mary on her dress for the Ball, and Mary insists on
her accepting a necklace to take the amber cross. She chooses a
gold one and is most confused when told it was a gift from
Henry to his sister. She is forced to accept it.

coze A friendly chat.

Chapter XXVII

On reaching home Fanny finds Edmund waiting for her with
the present of a gold chain for the cross. She is overwhelmed
with gratitude and wishes to return Mary Crawford's, but
Edmund prevents her, saying that he would not have any
coolness arise between the two dearest objects he had on earth.
When he has gone Fanny feels a stab at realizing what she has
long suspected: Edmund will marry Mary. Later Edmund
tells Fanny that he has been to the Parsonage to ask Mary for
the first two dances and is distressed at her reply that it will be
the last time, as she will not dance with a clergyman. He

despairs of marrying her. Fanny dresses for the Ball in a happy frame of mind.

travelling post . . . mail See *Travel*, p.8.

Chapter XXVIII

Sir Thomas is struck by Fanny's beauty at dinner before the Ball. The guests begin to arrive and the introductions are formal and rather frightening for Fanny. When the Crawfords arrive the preliminaries become less stiff, and Henry soon reserves the first two dances with Fanny. Sir Thomas insists on Fanny taking the floor first and the Ball begins. Fanny enjoys it but wishes that Henry were not so persistent in his attentions. Sir Thomas is happily convinced that Henry is in love with her. Edmund's evening is not happy. Mary again criticizes the clergy, and they part in mutual vexation. Fanny is eagerly sought as a partner and particularly enjoys her two dances with Edmund. At three o'clock Sir Thomas 'advises' Fanny to go to bed as she looks tired, and she goes, with the reflection that a Ball was indeed delightful.

à la mortal Imperfect.
the Lady of Branxholm Hall From Scott's *Lay of the Last Minstrel*.
negus Hot wine punch.

Chapter XXIX

William and Henry depart the next morning; also Edmund who goes to Peterborough for a week, during which he will be ordained. The house is very quiet without them. Julia writes and gains permission to stay in London with the Rushworths. At the Parsonage Mary misses Edmund greatly but is vexed by his defiance of her wishes in taking Orders. When he defers his homecoming, her vexation increases and also her remorse at having spoken unkindly of the clergy. She questions Fanny as to his movements and also discloses her jealousy when asking about the Miss Owens, daughters of the house at Peterborough.

con amore With love or zeal.

Chapter XXX

Henry Crawford returns to the Parsonage and tells his sister of his determination to marry Fanny. He praises her at length and his sister is delighted with his decision.

the sweep Curved carriage drive.
the pleasing plague Love. The line is quoted from a song.

Revision questions on Chapters XXI–XXX

1 Show how Henry's feelings for Fanny change from those of an idle flirtation to love.

2 Describe the dinner party at the Parsonage, and the card games that follow.

3 Write a letter from Fanny to her mother, describing the 'coming-out' Ball.

4 Give an account of the gifts of a necklace and a chain to Fanny.

5 What agitations did Fanny go through, due to the Ball?

Chapter XXXI

Henry informs Fanny of William's promotion to second lieutenant and of his journey to London, undertaken especially to introduce William to his uncle, the Admiral, and to persuade the latter to recommend him for a commission. Fanny is overjoyed and full of gratitude and Henry seizes the opportunity to propose to her. Fanny is astonished and believes he is trifling. When he persists, she retires in distress to her room and stays until he leaves the house. Henry comes to dinner that evening and brings a note from Mary urging Fanny to accept her brother. She is very distressed throughout dinner. Before he goes she gives him a note for Mary, begging her not to mention the subject again; and so ends a day of great pain and great pleasure for Fanny.

sloop A small ship-of-war, carrying guns on the upper deck only.
East Indies India and the islands beyond.

Chapter XXXII

The next morning Henry visits the Park and Fanny remains in her room. After half an hour Sir Thomas comes up. He notices with surprise that she has no fire and then tells her to sit down as he has something to say to her. He tells her of Henry's request for her hand in marriage and asks her to come down to meet him. Fanny exclaims that she cannot like him well enough to marry him. Sir Thomas is most surprised. He praises Henry's character and fortune and reminds her of his kindness to William. She still refuses, and when he upbraids her with cold severity for her wilfulness, obstinacy, selfishness and finally, ingratitude, Fanny cries bitterly, and Sir Thomas leaves her to her misery. He returns in a quarter of an hour to tell her that Henry has left but that he would like to see her for five minutes the next day. In the meanwhile, Sir Thomas advises her to take a walk and not to tell anyone what has passed. On her return she finds a fire in her room. At dinner Mrs Norris bullies her for going for a walk and not telling her. After dinner Sir Thomas leaves the room and then sends for Fanny. She goes to his room and finds herself alone with Henry.

Chapter XXXIII

Fanny tells Henry that she can never love him; but his vanity tells him that she will learn to, and her refusal merely strengthens his resolve. The next day Henry sees Sir Thomas and impresses him by his optimism. Sir Thomas tells Lady Bertram and Mrs Norris of the refusal; the former is gratified that a niece of hers should be honoured by such a proposal; the latter grudges any possible advance for a niece whom she has always tried to hold back.

Chapter XXXIV

Edmund returns. He is surprised to find Mary Crawford still at Mansfield, and more surprised by the friendly welcome she gives him. He speaks to Fanny about her refusal of Henry, and shows himself to be on his father's side in wishing the marriage. Henry dines at the Park, and, picking up a copy of Shakespeare's *Henry VIII* which Fanny has been reading to Lady Bertram, he reads several speeches aloud and receives great praise for his reading. This leads to a discussion with Edmund on reading aloud, and then to eloquence in the pulpit. Henry speaks of his envy of good preachers, declaring that he would like to be one himself, but only to preach occasionally. Fanny, who has been silent throughout, gives an involuntary shake of the head at this pronouncement. Henry eagerly tries to make her divulge her reason. She reproves him and he tells her of his determination to win her by the example of his constancy. The arrival of tea saves Fanny from further embarrassment.

Cardinal Wolsey A character from Shakespeare's *Henry VIII*, as are *The King*, *The Queen*, *Buckingham*, and *Cromwell* (the last being servant to Wolsey).
liturgy Form of worship.
tea-board Tea-tray.

Chapter XXXV

Edmund walks with Fanny in the shrubbery and talks to her about Henry. He defends her actions in refusing a man she does not love; but he urges her to try to love him. Fanny says it can never be as she and Henry are totally unlike. Edmund disagrees with this and quotes their literary tastes as a similarity. He admits their opposed temperaments – one cheerful, the other serious – but maintains that this is an aid to matrimonial happiness. Fanny then criticizes Henry's character, particularly with regard to his flirting with Maria. Edmund replies that the period of *Lovers' Vows* was one of general folly and that Henry was provoked by Maria. He again urges Fanny to love Henry and admits that he has a personal interest in the match. This turns the conversation on to Mary Crawford, and Edmund tells of her eagerness for the marriage and her inability to understand Fanny's refusal. Fanny answers that even if Henry were acceptable, he had taken her so much by surprise that she could not have returned an immediate affection. Edmund is encouraged by this to believe that it is simply a matter of time. Fanny looks tired and they return to the house.

Chapter XXXVI

Mary calls and asks Fanny to speak with her alone. They retire to the east room. Mary's memories of rehearsing with Edmund are awakened at the sight of the room, and after speaking of them she talks to Fanny about Henry, telling her what a sensation the news will make in London where so many young ladies have tried to catch him in vain. She tells Fanny that she cannot have been quite so surprised by his proposal as she had made out to Edmund, since Henry had been showing his affection for some time, and she gives as an example the gift of the necklace. Fanny is shocked to hear Mary confirm her recent suspicions that the gift was Henry's idea. Mary admits that Henry has been a flirt in the past, but assures Fanny that he is now completely serious. She then embraces Fanny, asks her to correspond with her in London, and departs. Henry comes in the evening also to say goodbye, and the next day the Crawfords depart.

exigeant Exacting.
The Blues The Regiment of Royal Horse Guards.

Chapter XXXVII

Sir Thomas hopes that Henry's absence may make Fanny fonder of him. Fanny again fears that Edmund will marry Mary, whom she considers unworthy of him, and she dreads his going to London shortly, when he will no doubt propose to Mary. William arrives, on ten-days' leave, and Sir Thomas arranges for Fanny to return to Portsmouth with him and visit her family. He hopes that the temporary loss of the luxuries of Mansfield would encourage her to seek a permanent home with Henry. Fanny and William are delighted with the idea of returning together. At the last moment, to their horror, Mrs Norris considers accompanying them, but the thought of having to pay her fare back deters her. Edmund unselfishly postpones his journey to London to be with his parents. Fanny and William depart.

travelling post See *Travel*, p.8.

Chapter XXXVIII

The journey by post to Portmouth affords ample opportunity for pleasant talk. Passing through Oxford, they stay the night at Newbury and arrive at Portsmouth before dark on the next day. Eleven-year-old Sam greets them at the Prices' house with the news that the *Thrush* has left the harbour, is expecting her sailing orders shortly and that William is awaited. Fanny's mother greets her kindly, and she meets her sisters, Susan aged fourteen and Betsey aged five. She is taken into the parlour – so small a room that she mistakes it for a passage – and Mrs Price sends for tea. Mr Price comes in and, excitedly punctuating his speech with oaths, tells William of the *Thrush*'s movements. He greets Fanny, who is pained by the oaths and smell of spirits, then ignores her in favour of her brother. After some time a candle is brought, but still no tea. Two more brothers, aged eight and nine, come in from school, and this completes the family, except for two absent brothers, one a clerk in London, the other a midshipman at sea. Fanny is almost stunned by the noise and muddle, and her head aches as she sits with her father who ignores her and reads the paper. She cannot help comparing it adversely with Mansfield. At last tea arrives, and to Fanny's delight William comes down in his uniform. After tea William goes to join his ship and his brothers see him off. Mr Price also goes out, and Mrs Price, after asking Fanny a few questions about Mansfield, turns to her favourite conversation, the servant problem. Susan and Betsey quarrel over a silver knife. Very tired, Fanny retires to the tiny bedroom she is to share with Susan. Downstairs the confusion and noise continue.

the *Texel* A Dutch island, scene of the surrender of their fleet to Admiral Mitchell, 1799.
eight-and-twenty A ship carrying twenty-eight guns, i.e. a frigate which was larger than a sloop but smaller than a ship of the line.
the sheer-hulk An old ship fitted with sheers which were used for hoisting.

Chapter XXXIX

Before the end of a week Fanny is very disappointed in her home. William has sailed and with him Sam, thanks to Fanny's efforts to prepare his kit. She finds her father swears and drinks, and is dirty and gross, and neglects his family. Her mother is not unkind, but she has little idea of managing the house or her children and little interest in Fanny. The result is an abode of incessant noise and disorder, forming such a contrast in Fanny's mind to her former life that she yearns for Mansfield Park.

Dr Johnson's celebrated judgement 'Marriage has many pains, but celibacy has no pleasures.'

Chapter XL

Fanny, in her 'exile', welcomes a letter from Mary Crawford. She writes that Henry has gone to Norfolk, that she has visited the Rushworths and that Maria was shaken by the news of Henry's love for Fanny. The Rushworths are shortly to occupy a very fine house in London. Mr Yates continues his attentions to Julia, though Maria does not consider him much of a 'catch'. Edmund has not yet visited her in London. Fanny finds consolation in befriending Susan. She settles the quarrel between her and Betsey by buying the latter a silver knife for herself, and so gains the respect of Susan. An intimacy grows between them and they spend the mornings together. Fanny helps Susan to improve both her manners and her mind, and at the same time escapes the confusion downstairs. Fanny joins a circulating library to encourage Susan to read. A letter from Aunt Bertram brings news that Edmund has gone to London. Fanny dreads the postman's next knock.

Baron Wildenheim's attentions John Yates, who took that part in *Lovers' Vows* and ranted his way through the play.
pelisses Long mantles of silk, velvet, or cloth.
in propria persona In her own person.

Revision questions on Chapters XXXI–XL

1 Give an account of Henry's courtship of Fanny at Mansfield.

2 Summarize Sir Thomas's interview with Fanny on the subject of Henry's proposal.

3 What are Edmund's views on Henry's proposal, and how far are they influenced by his own interests?

4 Give a detailed account of the Prices' home at Portsmouth.

5 Why is Fanny disappointed in her father and mother?

Chapter XLI

Nearly four weeks after Fanny's arrival at Portsmouth, Henry Crawford pays a surprise visit. When Fanny has recovered from the shock, and after introducing him to her mother as a friend of William, Henry takes her and Susan for a walk. To her distress they meet Mr Price, but to Fanny's relief he behaves in a well-mannered way and takes them all to visit the dockyard. There he wanders off with a friend and Henry and the girls take a rest. Henry tells Fanny about his affairs in Norfolk, impressing her with his benevolence towards some tenants. After speaking fondly of Mansfield, he tells her he has come to Portsmouth for two days especially to be with her. Though she regrets this she cannot help feeling that he has greatly improved. Fortunately for Fanny's peace of mind, he refuses an invitation to dinner at the Prices' and arranges to meet them next day.

the island The Isle of Wight.
eulogium A speech of praise.
hunting-box A small country-house from which to hunt.

Chapter XLII

The second day of his visit being Sunday, Henry goes to the garrison chapel with the Prices, and joins them in their customary walk on the ramparts after the service. He walks arm in arm with Fanny and Susan, and though this embarrasses Fanny for a time, she soon welcomes it when she tires. It is a lovely day and they admire the beauty of the sea. Henry notices that Fanny does not look so well as she did at Mansfield and promises to come with his sister and fetch her back to Mansfield if only she will write directly she feels unwell. Henry tells Fanny he has half a mind to return to Norfolk and complete some business on his estate. They say goodbye and Fanny returns to an unattractive lunch at home. She cannot help admitting that Henry has improved wonderfully and hopes he may soon discontinue his distressing attentions to her.

Chapter XLIII

Two days later Fanny receives a letter from Mary Crawford telling her how much Henry had enjoyed his visit to Portsmouth. She tells of the parties she has had in London, and mentions seeing Edmund two or three times. Henry, she mentions, may go on to Norfolk, but he is to stay in London for a party they are giving and to which the Rushworths have been invited. Fanny realizes from this letter that Edmund has not yet proposed and wonders if Mary's feelings for him will change. She considers her arrangement of a meeting between Henry and the Rushworths most ill-judged. She anxiously awaits a letter from Edmund, but none comes. Meanwhile Susan proves a keen pupil and grows very fond of Fanny.

St George's, Hanover Square A fashionable church for society weddings.
Goldsmith Poet, novelist, and playwright, 1730–74.

Chapter XLIV

After nearly seven weeks at Portsmouth, the long-awaited letter from Edmund arrives. He found Mary very altered in London and ascribes it to the influence of mercenary Mrs Fraser. Nevertheless, he affirms that Mary is the only woman he could ever marry, though he doubts if he will win her. He closes his letter by stating that Sir Thomas means to fetch Fanny himself, but not until after Easter. Fanny is most disappointed that her return to Mansfield is to be postponed, and half angry with Edmund for delaying his proposal to Mary, and thus prolonging the suspense. A few days later Lady Bertram writes and tells of Tom Bertram's serious illness at Newmarket. Edmund is to fetch him back to Mansfield. Fanny feels greatly for all at Mansfield. Lady Bertram writes regularly and soon reports that Tom is home but that the journey has made him worse.

Chapter XLV

Edmund writes to tell Fanny that though Tom's fever is better, the physician fears for his lungs. Edmund has abandoned the idea of proposing to Mary by letter and will visit her when Tom is better. Easter comes and still Fanny is left at Portsmouth, longing for the country and anxious to help the Bertrams. Mary writes eagerly asking Fanny the latest news of Tom's illness, and not disguising her selfish interest in the possibility of Edmund inheriting the title and the estate. She mentions that Henry has been staying at Richmond and seeing Maria. She again offers to fetch Fanny to Mansfield. Fanny is disgusted with Mary's cold-hearted ambition and Henry's thoughtless vanity, and, much as she wishes to return, she refuses Mary's offer of fetching her.

Cowper's *Tirocinium* William Cowper, poet, 1731–1800. His *Tirocinium* was a vigorous attack on public schools.

Chapter XLVI

A week later a letter comes from Mary Crawford, telling of the rumour of an indiscretion in which Henry and Maria are involved. Fanny is anxious and bewildered. The following evening her father shows her a report in the newspaper: Maria has left her husband and run away with Henry. Fanny is stupefied; she thinks of all the misery that will fall on each of the Bertrams. Edmund writes from London to say they cannot trace Henry and Maria and that another blow has fallen: Julia has eloped to Scotland with John Yates. Edmund is coming to fetch Fanny, and Susan is to accompany her and to stay at Mansfield for a few months. Fanny's feelings are mixed; she is delighted to be returning, but shocked by the additional news of Julia. She finds plenty to do preparing Susan and herself for the journey. Edmund arrives and within half an hour they leave with him on the silent journey to Mansfield. Breaking the journey at Oxford, they reach Mansfield on the second day, a full three months since Fanny left there.

étourderie Thoughtlessness.
fracas Disturbance.

Chapter XLVII

Lady Bertram is delighted to have Fanny back. Mrs Norris is an altered creature; Maria had been her favourite and the match her own contriving and the events have stupefied her. Lady Bertram tells Fanny the full story. Maria had stayed with friends at Twickenham for Easter whilst her husband went to Bath to fetch his mother. It appears that Henry had access to the friends' house at all times. Then Sir Thomas had received a letter from an old friend in London, telling him of an unpleasant rumour about Maria's behaviour, and he was about to act when a further letter, describing a worsening situation, arrived. Maria had left her husband and Mrs Rushworth senior was being extremely difficult. Sir Thomas and Edmund went to London at once, but all had become public and Henry and Maria had vanished. Sir Thomas stays in the hope of finding them. Three days after Fanny's return, Edmund tells her of his meeting with Mary Crawford in London. He had gone prepared to find her full of shame for her brother; instead Mary talks of their 'folly', particularly in being detected, and deplores the fact that Henry has thrown away his chances of Fanny. She speaks of marriage between Henry and Maria as the only remaining remedy. This acquiescence in sin is a further shock to Edmund. His eyes are now open to her lack of principle. Fanny's friendship was all that he had to cling to.

Methodists See under *The clergy*, p.6.

Chapter XLVIII

Fanny is happy. Sir Thomas understands her refusal of Henry. Edmund is no longer duped by Mary. Sir Thomas blames himself for the disaster in allowing Mary to marry Rushworth; but he finds comfort in Julia, who wishes to be forgiven, and in her husband, who is now anxious to please. Tom improves in health and character. Mr Rushworth procures a divorce, and Maria lives with Henry until they hate each other, then she goes to live with Mrs Norris in another county and their tempers become their mutual punishment. Henry Crawford suffers remorse for throwing away his chances of marrying Fanny. The Grants, fortunately, leave Mansfield for London and Mary makes her home with them, and lives with Mrs Grant after the Doctor's death. In time, Edmund falls in love with Fanny and, as Lady Bertram is now able to spare Fanny since she has Susan as a permanent comforter, they marry and, after Dr Grant's death, settle at Mansfield Parsonage, much to Sir Thomas's delight and Fanny's joy.

Revision questions on Chapters XLI–XLVIII

1 What improvements do you find in Henry on his visit to Portsmouth?

2 Give a summary of Edmund's first letter to Fanny at Portsmouth.

3 Tell the whole story of Maria's and Julia's elopements.

4 Describe Edmund's last interview with Mary Crawford.

5 What happens to each of the main characters at the end of the story?

General questions

1 Compare the everyday life at Mansfield Park with that at the Prices' house in Portsmouth.

2 What have you learnt from the novel of English life at the close of the eighteenth century?

3 What have you learnt about houses and gardens, and the various attempts to 'improve' them?

4 What does the novel tell you about (a) education, (b) entertainment in those days?

5 It is easy to admire Fanny for her goodness, and to sympathize with her in her troubles, but it is not easy to love her for herself. Comment on this statement.

6 Compare the characters of two of the following sisters: Lady Bertram, Mrs Norris, Mrs Price.

7 What light do the preparations for *Lovers' Vows* throw on each of the characters involved?

8 Do you find Edmund Bertram attractive, or not? Give full reasons for your verdict.

9 Henry Crawford shows two very opposed sides to his nature in the story. Comment on them both.

10 'Hers are faults of principle, Fanny – of blunted delicacy and a corrupted mind.' Discuss the justice, or otherwise, of this criticism of Mary Crawford by Edmund.

11 'Unintelligibly moral, so infamously tyrannical.' Attempt to defend Sir Thomas Bertram against this scathing criticism by Mr Yates.

12 Discuss the accomplishments and characters of the two Miss Bertrams.

13 Show that the minor characters possess an individuality and are cleverly drawn, by referring to four of the following: Tom Bertram, James Rushworth, John Yates, William Price, Mr Price, Mrs Price, Dr Grant.

14 What are the main characteristics of Jane Austen's style? Illustrate your answer with examples from *Mansfield Park*.

15 'She knew what she wanted to do, and within the limits she set herself, she achieved perfection.' What were these 'limits', and do you find they detract from the enjoyment of the novel?

Context questions

Answer briefly the questions below each of the following passages.

1 'If that be all your difficulty, I will furnish you with paper and every other material, and you may write your letter whenever you choose.'

a Who spoke these words, and to whom?
b To whom was the letter to be written?
c On what occasion is it spoken, and what does it tell you of the speaker's character?

2 'If I had known this before, I would have spoken of the cloth with more respect.'

a Who says this, and where is the speaker when it is said?
b What had the speaker been saying about 'the cloth'?
c What was it that she had just learned?

3 'It would show great want of feeling on my father's account, absent as he is, and in some degree of constant danger.'

a Who speaks these words, and to whom?
b What would show great want of feeling?
c What light does this passage throw on the speaker's character?

4 'My dear Sir Thomas, if you had seen the state of the roads *that* day!'

a Who speaks and on what occasion?
b Give a brief account of the journey undertaken on *that* day.

5 'My uncle, who is the very best man in the world, has exerted himself, as I knew he would after seeing your brother.'

a Who speaks and to whom?

b What has his uncle done for the brother?

c The speaker uses this news to introduce other and, to him, more important business. What was the business?

6 'Perhaps, sir,' said Fanny, wearied at last into speaking – 'perhaps, sir, I thought it was a pity you did not always know yourself as well as you seemed to do at that moment.'

a To whom is Fanny speaking?

b What had he just said which led Fanny to believe that he knew himself well at that moment?

7 'I put it to your conscience whether "Sir Edmund" would not do more good with all the Bertram property than any other possible "sir".'

a Who wrote these words, and on what occasion?

b On what does the writer base hopes of Edmund having all the Bertram property?

c What does this passage tell us of the writer's character.

8 She passed only from feelings of sickness to shudderings of horror; and from hot fits of fever to cold. The event was so shocking that there were moments when her heart revolted from it as impossible, when she thought it could not be.

a What was so shocking?

b How did Fanny first hear of the shocking event?

c What other shocking news does she hear very shortly afterwards, and who informs her of it?

9 'MY DEAR FANNY, – I take up my pen to communicate some very alarming intelligence, which I make no doubt will give you much concern.'

a Who wrote this letter to Fanny?

b Where was Fanny when she received it?

c What is the alarming intelligence, and how did it come about?

10 '. . . it is of all parts in the world the most disgusting to me. I quite detest her. An odious, little, pert, unnatural, impudent girl. I have always protested against comedy, and this is comedy in its worst form.'

a Who is speaking?
b Why is she angry?
c Name the chosen play, and make a list of the characters and the players.

Connect the following passages with their contexts and add comments on any points of interest.

11 'And how do you think I mean to amuse myself, Mary, on the days that I do not hunt? I am grown too old to go out more than three times a week; but I have a plan for the intermediate days, and what do you think it is?'

12 'It wants improvement, ma'am, beyond anything. I never saw a place that wanted so much improvement in my life; and it is so forlorn that I do not know what can be done with it.'

13 The elegance, propriety, regularity, harmony, and perhaps, above all the peace and tranquillity of Mansfield, were brought to her remembrance every hour of the day, by the prevalence of everything opposite to them *here*.

14 The former was on the barouche box in a moment, the latter took her seat within, in gloom and mortification; and the carriage drove off amid the good wishes of the two remaining ladies, and the barking of Pug in his mistress's arms.

15 'You have proved yourself upright and disinterested: prove yourself grateful and tender-hearted; and then you will be the perfect model of a woman, which I have always believed you born for.'

16 'I am fairly caught. You know with what idle designs I began; but this is the end of them. I have (I flatter myself) made no inconsiderable progress in her affections, but my own are entirely fixed.'

17 Such a victory over Edmund's discretion had been beyond their hopes, and was most delightful. There was no longer anything to disturb them in their darling project, and they congratulated each other in private on the jealous weakness to which they attributed the change, with all the glee of feelings gratified in every way.

18 William and Fanny were horror-struck at the idea. All the comfort of their comfortable journey would be destroyed at once. With woeful countenances they looked at each other. Their suspense lasted an hour or two. No one interfered to encourage or dissuade.

19 'Had she been different when I did see her, I should have made no complaint; but from the very first she was altered. My first reception was so unlike what I had hoped, that I had almost resolved on leaving London again directly.'

20 'But this morning we heard of it in the right way. It was seen by some farmer, and he told the miller, and the miller told the butcher, and the butcher's son-in-law left word at the shop.'

Key to context questions

1 II; **2** IX; **3** XIII; **4** XX; **5** XXXI; **6** XXXIV; **7** XLV;
8 XLVI; **9** XLIV; **10** XIV; **11** XXIV; **12** VI; **13** XXXIX;
14 VIII; **15** XXXV; **16** XXX; **17** XVII; **18** XXXVII;
19 XLIV; **20** VI.